STAR WARS

THE CLONE WARS

CRASH COURSE

DESIGNER **KRYSTAL HENNES**

ASSISTANT EDITOR **FREDDYE LINS**

ASSOCIATE EDITOR **DAVE MARSHALL**

EDITOR **RANDY STRADLEY**

PUBLISHER **MIKE RICHARDSON**

Special thanks to Elaine Mederer, Jann Moorhead, David Anderman, Leland Chee, Sue Rostoni, and Carol Roeder at Lucas Licensing.

Published by Dark Horse Books, a division of Dark Horse Comics, Inc.
10956 SE Main Street, Milwaukie, OR 97222

darkhorse.com | starwars.com

To find a comics shop in your area, call the Comic Shop Locator Service toll-free at 1.888.266.4226
First edition: December 2008 | ISBN 978-1-59582-230-7

10 9 8 7 6 5 4 3 2
Printed in Canada

 The events in these stories take place sometime during the Clone Wars.

STAR WARS: THE CLONE WARS—CRASH COURSE

STAR WARS

THE CLONE WARS

CRASH COURSE

STORY **HENRY GILROY & GARY SCHEPPKE**

SCRIPT **HENRY GILROY**

COLORS **RONDA PATTISON**

ART **THE FILLBACH BROTHERS**

LETTERING **MICHAEL HEISLER**

COVER ART **RAMÓN K. PÉREZ**

DARK HORSE BOOKS®

THIS STORY TAKES PLACE IN THE EARLY MONTHS OF THE CLONE WARS.

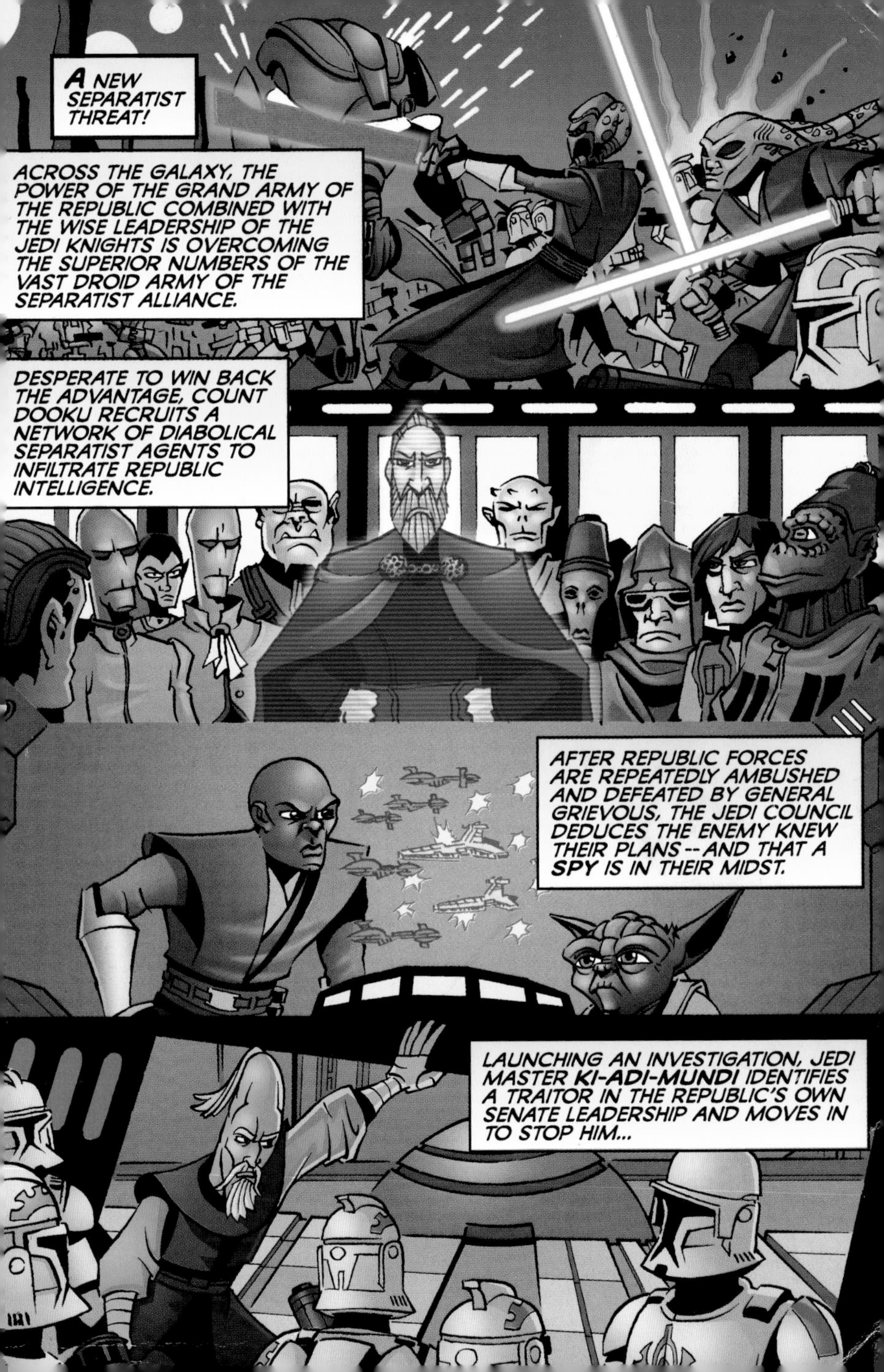
A NEW SEPARATIST THREAT!
ACROSS THE GALAXY, THE POWER OF THE GRAND ARMY OF THE REPUBLIC COMBINED WITH THE WISE LEADERSHIP OF THE JEDI KNIGHTS IS OVERCOMING THE SUPERIOR NUMBERS OF THE VAST DROID ARMY OF THE SEPARATIST ALLIANCE.
DESPERATE TO WIN BACK THE ADVANTAGE, COUNT DOOKU RECRUITS A NETWORK OF DIABOLICAL SEPARATIST AGENTS TO INFILTRATE REPUBLIC INTELLIGENCE.
AFTER REPUBLIC FORCES ARE REPEATEDLY AMBUSHED AND DEFEATED BY GENERAL GRIEVOUS, THE JEDI COUNCIL DEDUCES THE ENEMY KNEW THEIR PLANS--AND THAT A SPY IS IN THEIR MIDST.
LAUNCHING AN INVESTIGATION, JEDI MASTER KI-ADI-MUNDI IDENTIFIES A TRAITOR IN THE REPUBLIC'S OWN SENATE LEADERSHIP AND MOVES IN TO STOP HIM...

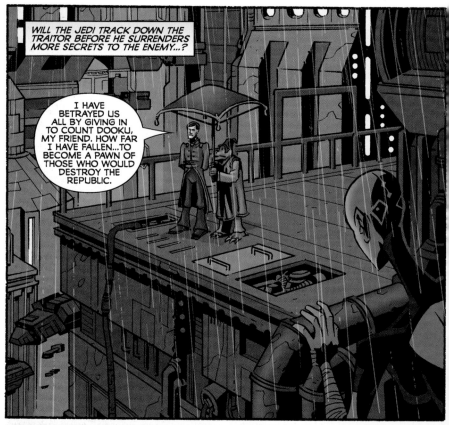

WILL THE JEDI TRACK DOWN THE TRAITOR BEFORE HE SURRENDERS MORE SECRETS TO THE ENEMY...?

I HAVE BETRAYED US ALL BY GIVING IN TO COUNT DOOKU, MY FRIEND. HOW FAR I HAVE FALLEN...TO BECOME A PAWN OF THOSE WHO WOULD DESTROY THE REPUBLIC.

YOU DID NOT HAVE A CHOICE, SENATOR. YOU MUST COOPERATE WITH THEM.

I KNOW YOU ARE RIGHT, MESSO...AT LEAST I CAN TRUST YOU.

WE SHOULD ALL BE SO FORTUNATE...

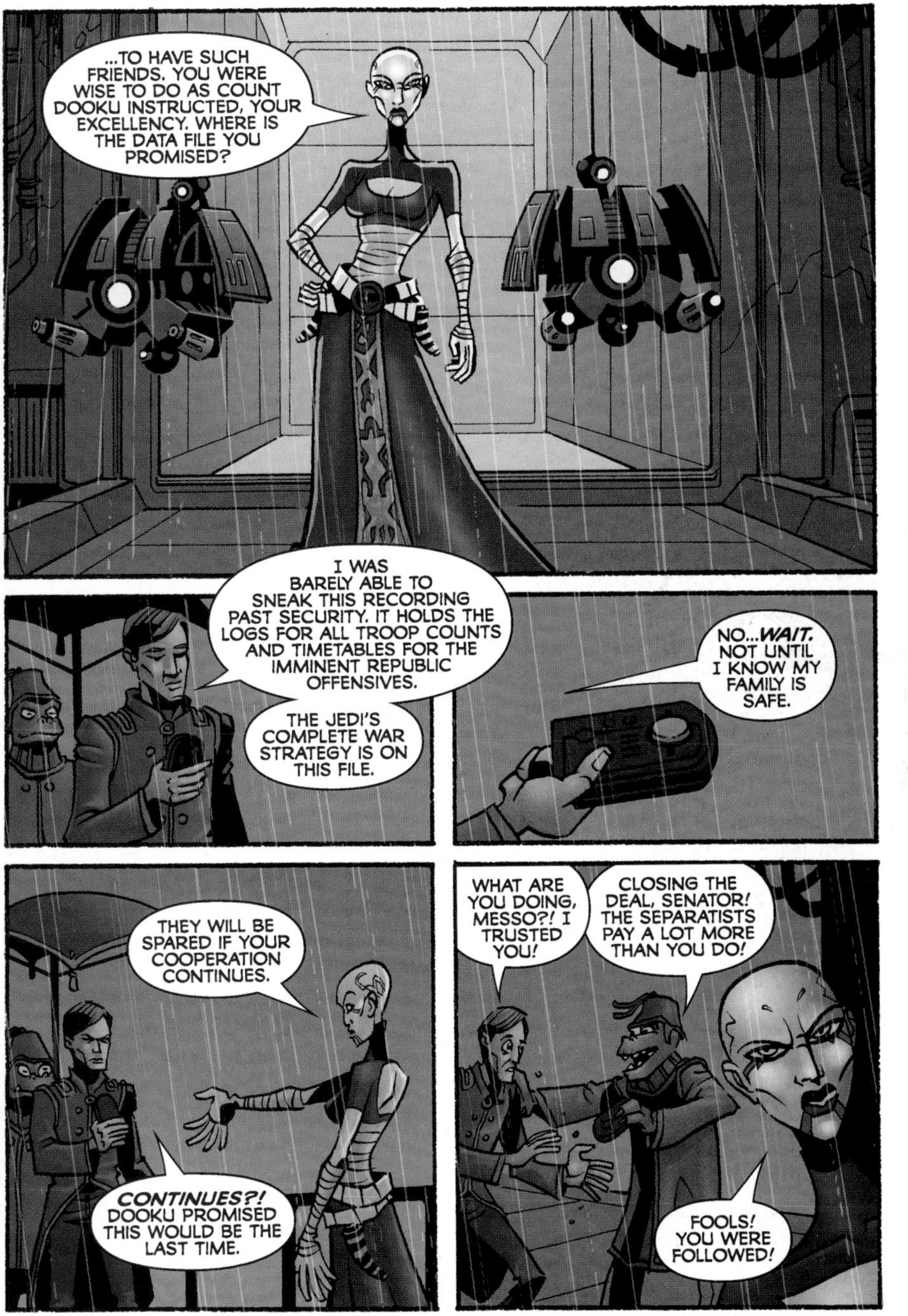
...TO HAVE SUCH FRIENDS. YOU WERE WISE TO DO AS COUNT DOOKU INSTRUCTED, YOUR EXCELLENCY. WHERE IS THE DATA FILE YOU PROMISED?
I WAS BARELY ABLE TO SNEAK THIS RECORDING PAST SECURITY. IT HOLDS THE LOGS FOR ALL TROOP COUNTS AND TIMETABLES FOR THE IMMINENT REPUBLIC OFFENSIVES.
THE JEDI'S COMPLETE WAR STRATEGY IS ON THIS FILE.
NO...*WAIT.* NOT UNTIL I KNOW MY FAMILY IS SAFE.
THEY WILL BE SPARED IF YOUR COOPERATION CONTINUES.
CONTINUES?! DOOKU PROMISED THIS WOULD BE THE LAST TIME.
WHAT ARE YOU DOING, MESSO?! I TRUSTED YOU!
CLOSING THE DEAL, SENATOR! THE SEPARATISTS PAY A LOT MORE THAN YOU DO!
FOOLS! YOU WERE FOLLOWED!

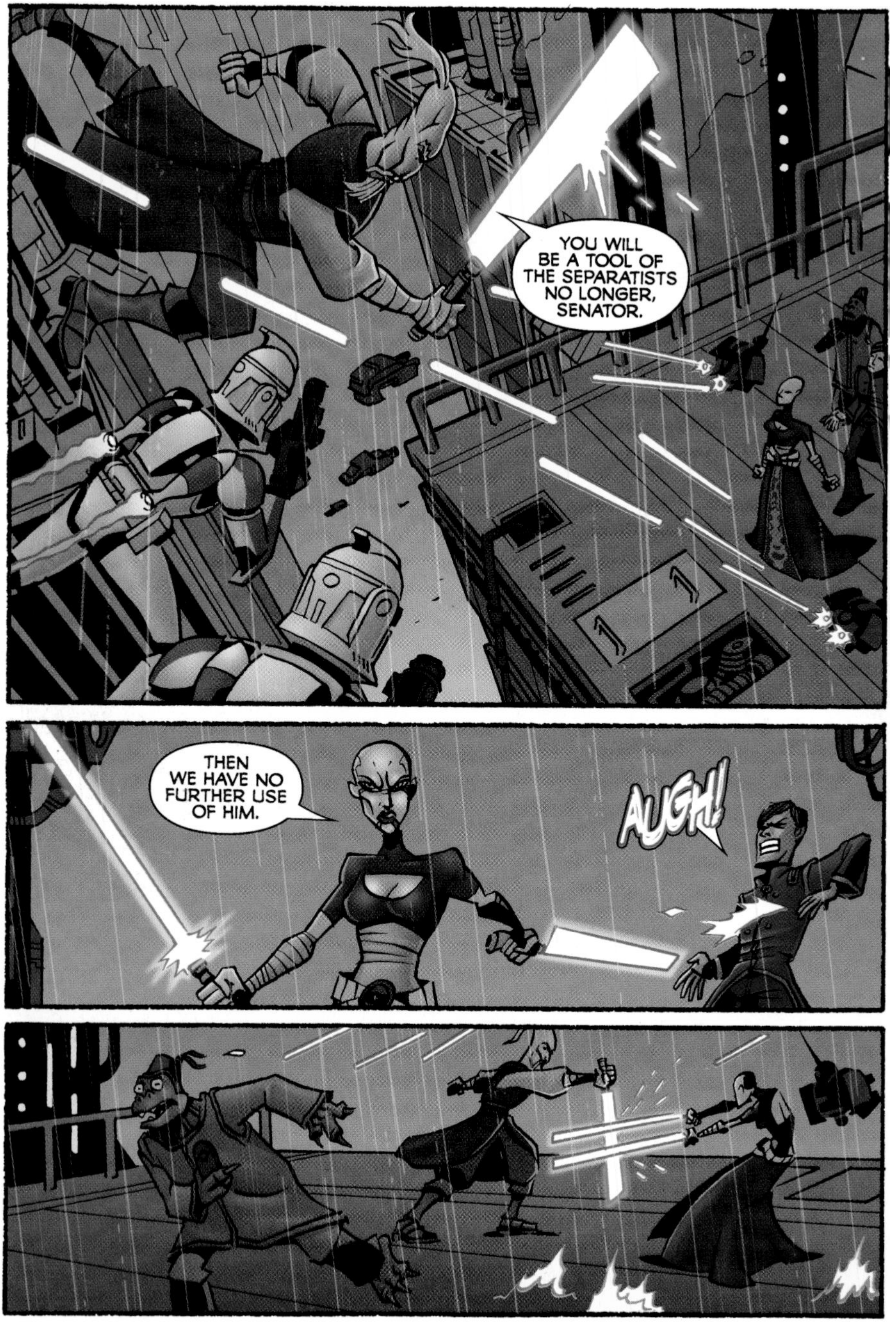
YOU WILL BE A TOOL OF THE SEPARATISTS NO LONGER, SENATOR.
THEN WE HAVE NO FURTHER USE OF HIM.
AUGH!

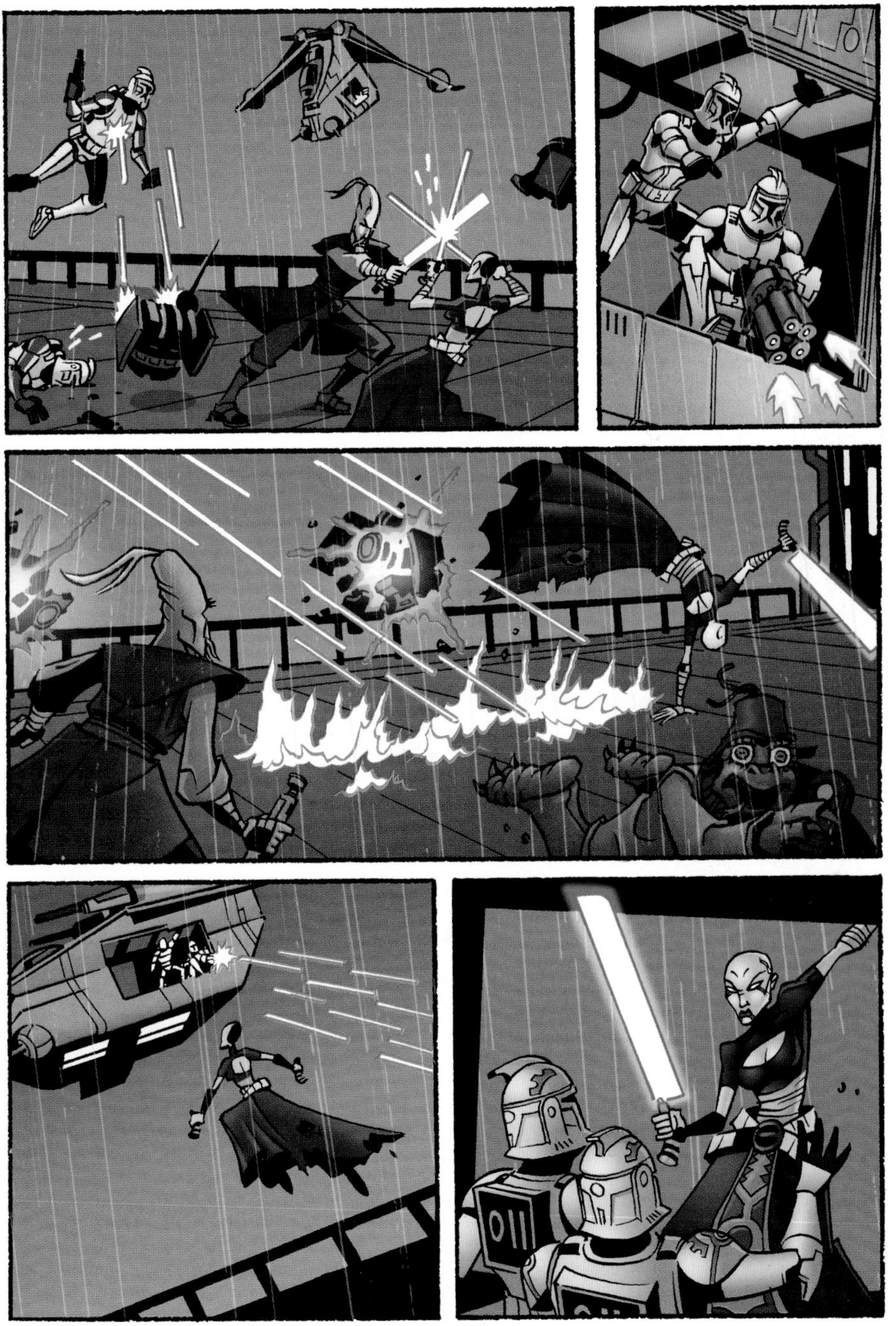

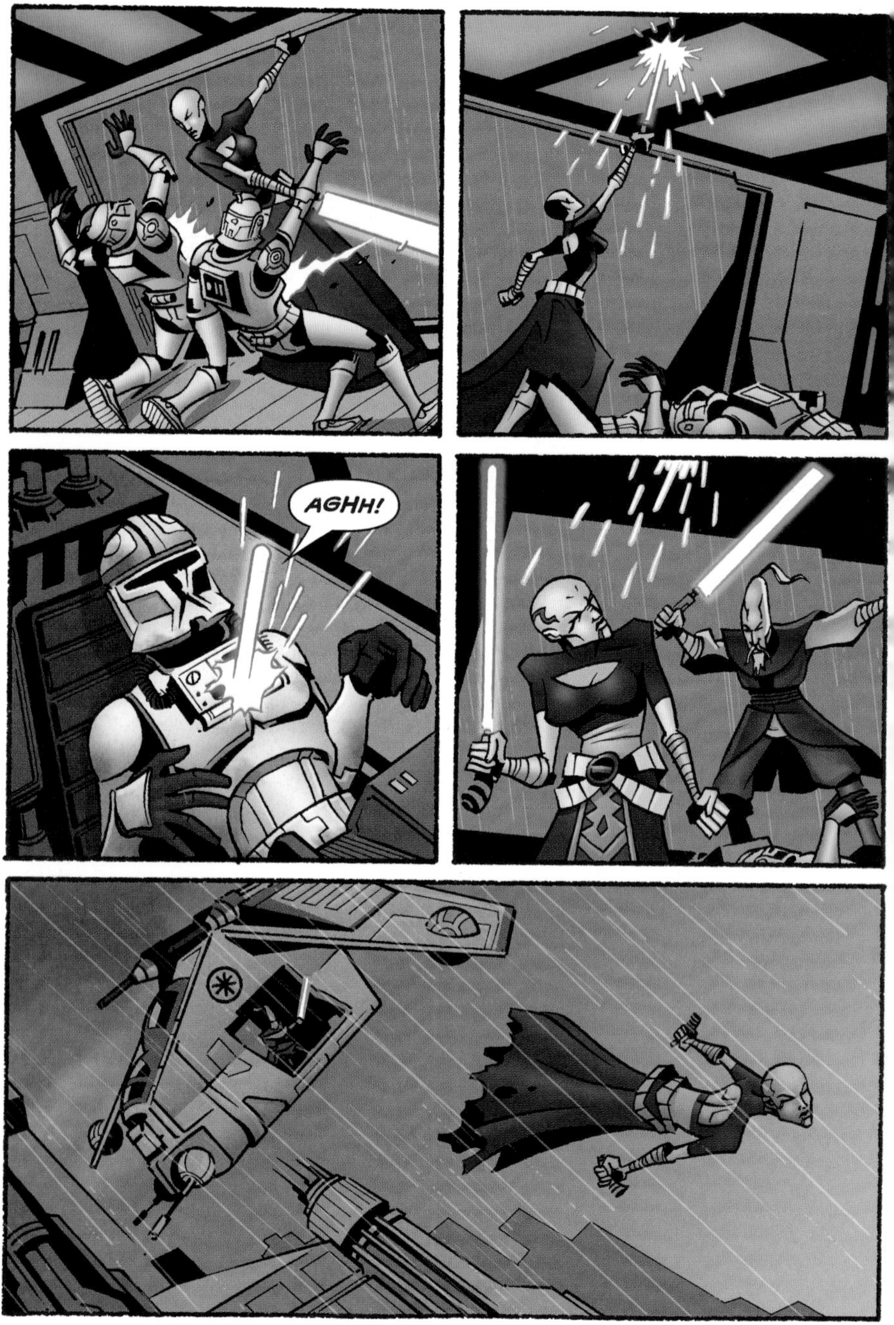
AGHH!

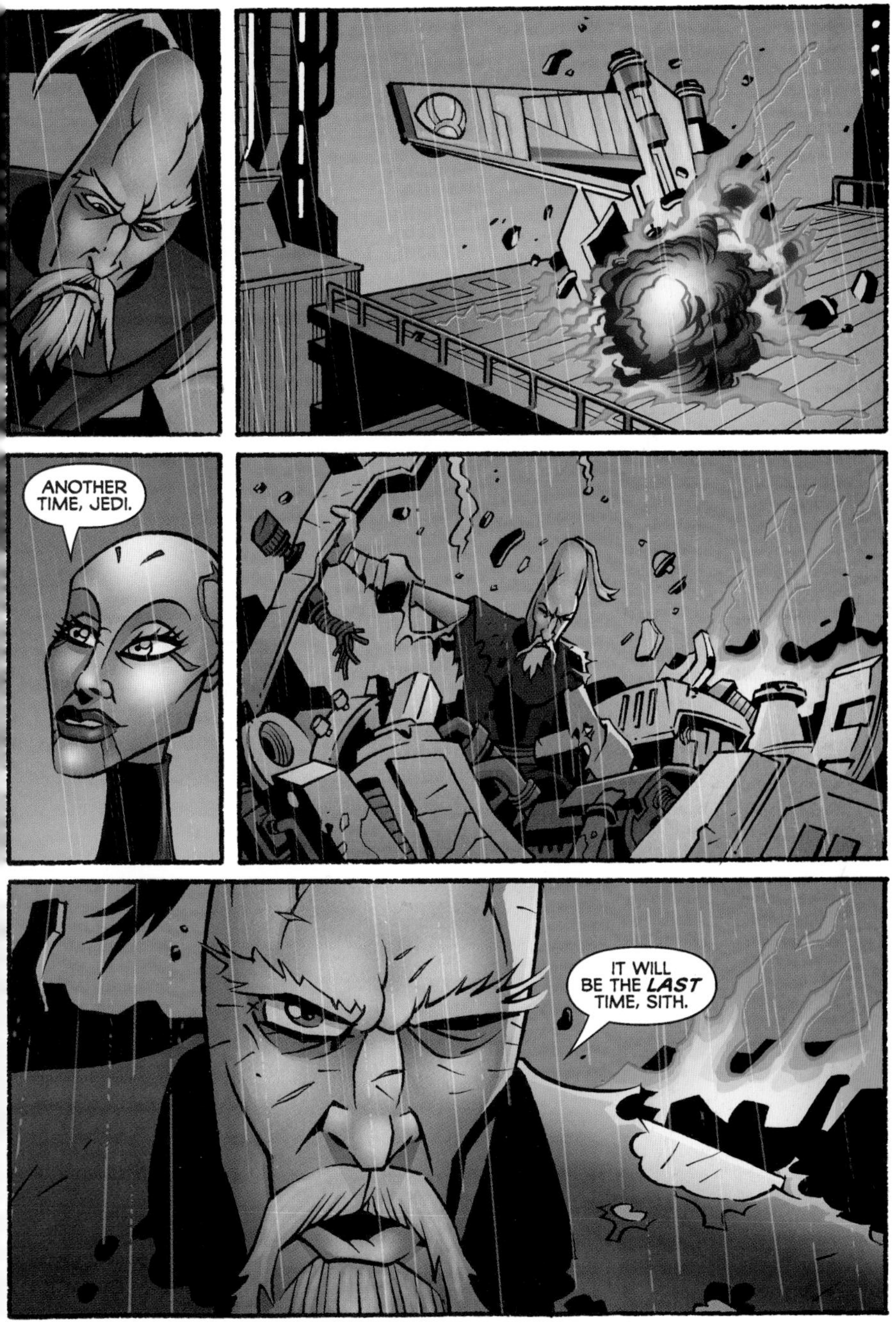
ANOTHER TIME, JEDI.
IT WILL BE THE *LAST* TIME, SITH.

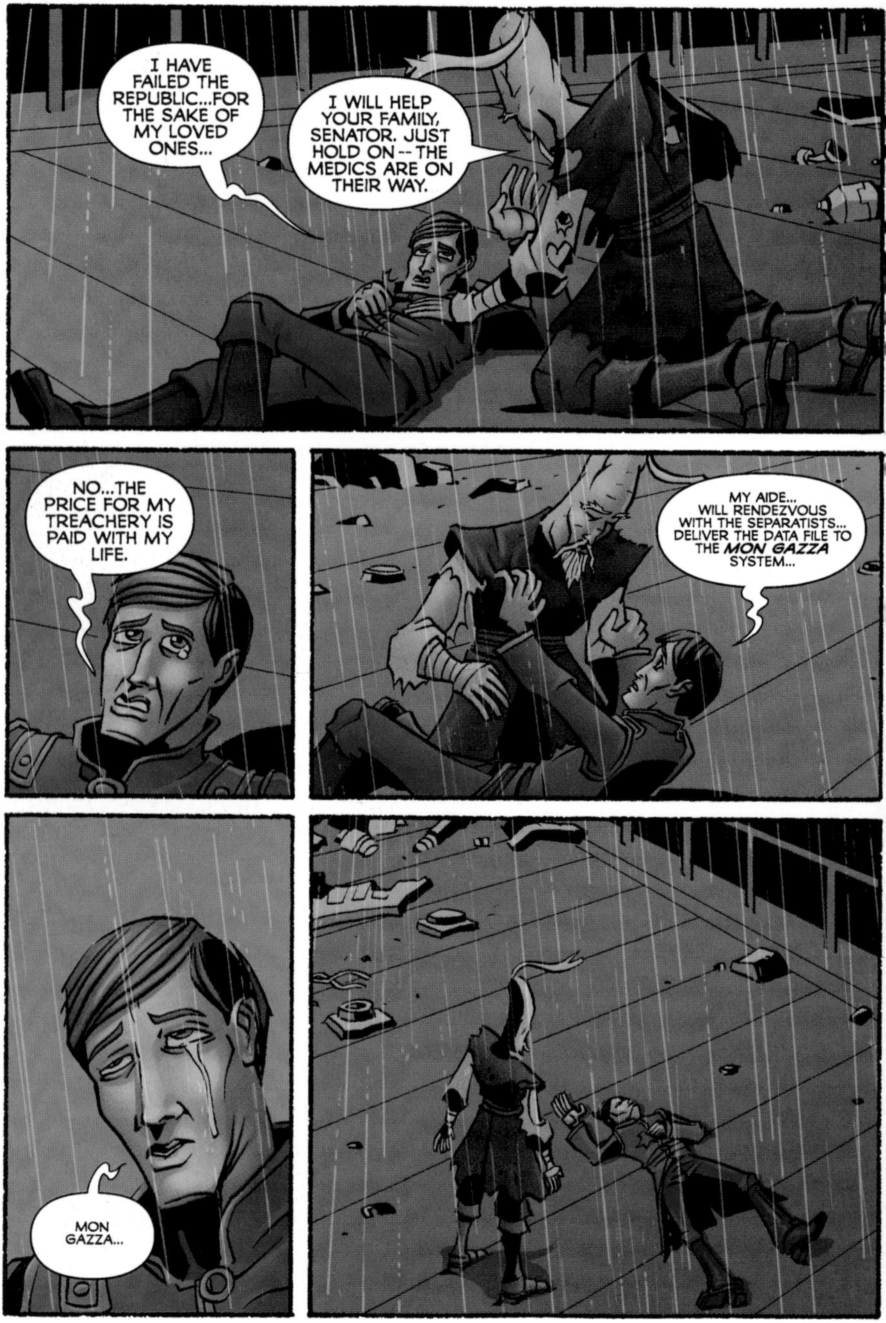
I HAVE FAILED THE REPUBLIC...FOR THE SAKE OF MY LOVED ONES...
I WILL HELP YOUR FAMILY, SENATOR. JUST HOLD ON -- THE MEDICS ARE ON THEIR WAY.
NO...THE PRICE FOR MY TREACHERY IS PAID WITH MY LIFE.
MY AIDE... WILL RENDEZVOUS WITH THE SEPARATISTS... DELIVER THE DATA FILE TO THE *MON GAZZA* SYSTEM...
MON GAZZA...

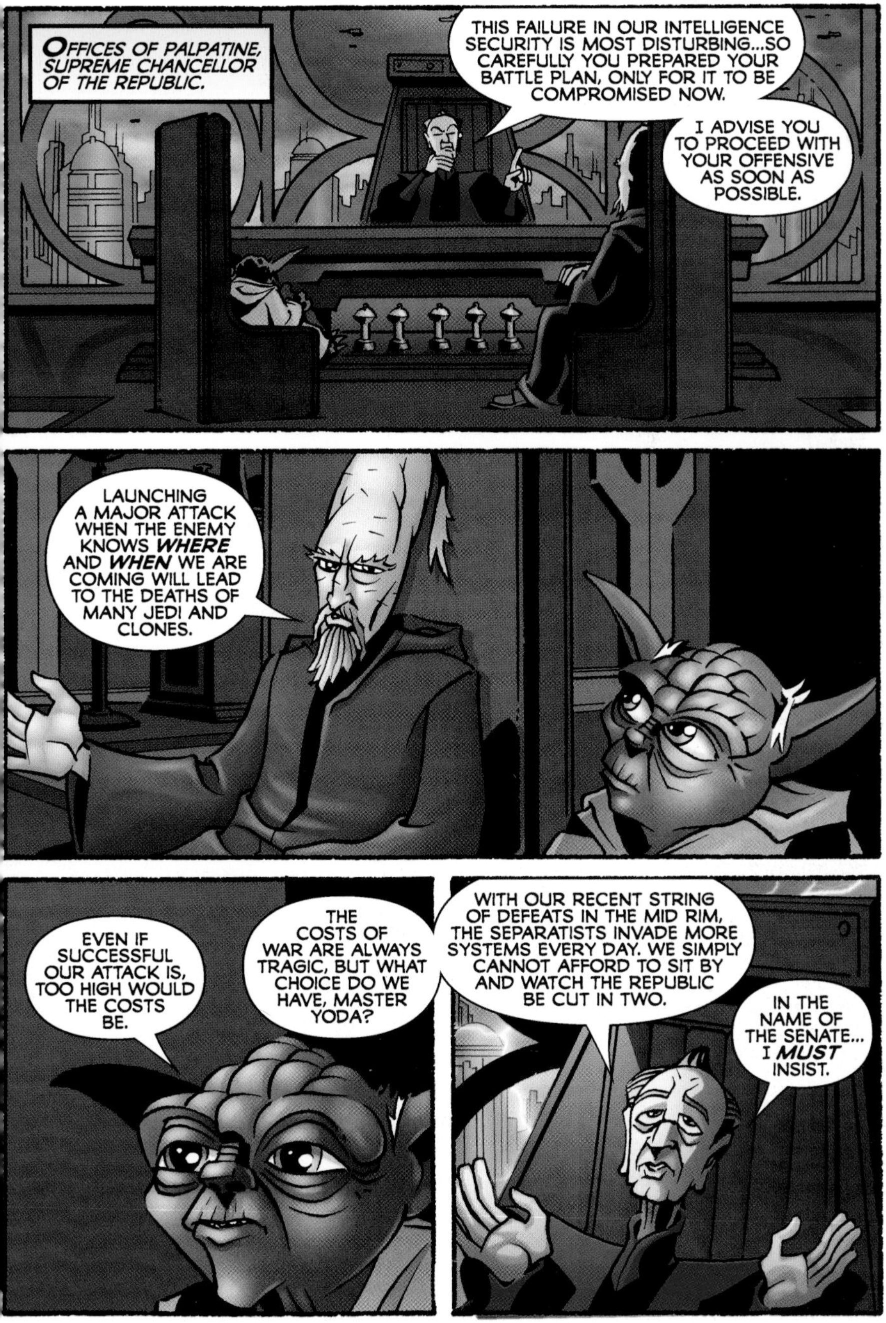
OFFICES OF PALPATINE, SUPREME CHANCELLOR OF THE REPUBLIC.
THIS FAILURE IN OUR INTELLIGENCE SECURITY IS MOST DISTURBING...SO CAREFULLY YOU PREPARED YOUR BATTLE PLAN, ONLY FOR IT TO BE COMPROMISED NOW.
I ADVISE YOU TO PROCEED WITH YOUR OFFENSIVE AS SOON AS POSSIBLE.
LAUNCHING A MAJOR ATTACK WHEN THE ENEMY KNOWS *WHERE* AND *WHEN* WE ARE COMING WILL LEAD TO THE DEATHS OF MANY JEDI AND CLONES.
EVEN IF SUCCESSFUL OUR ATTACK IS, TOO HIGH WOULD THE COSTS BE.
THE COSTS OF WAR ARE ALWAYS TRAGIC, BUT WHAT CHOICE DO WE HAVE, MASTER YODA?
WITH OUR RECENT STRING OF DEFEATS IN THE MID RIM, THE SEPARATISTS INVADE MORE SYSTEMS EVERY DAY. WE SIMPLY CANNOT AFFORD TO SIT BY AND WATCH THE REPUBLIC BE CUT IN TWO.
IN THE NAME OF THE SENATE... I *MUST* INSIST.

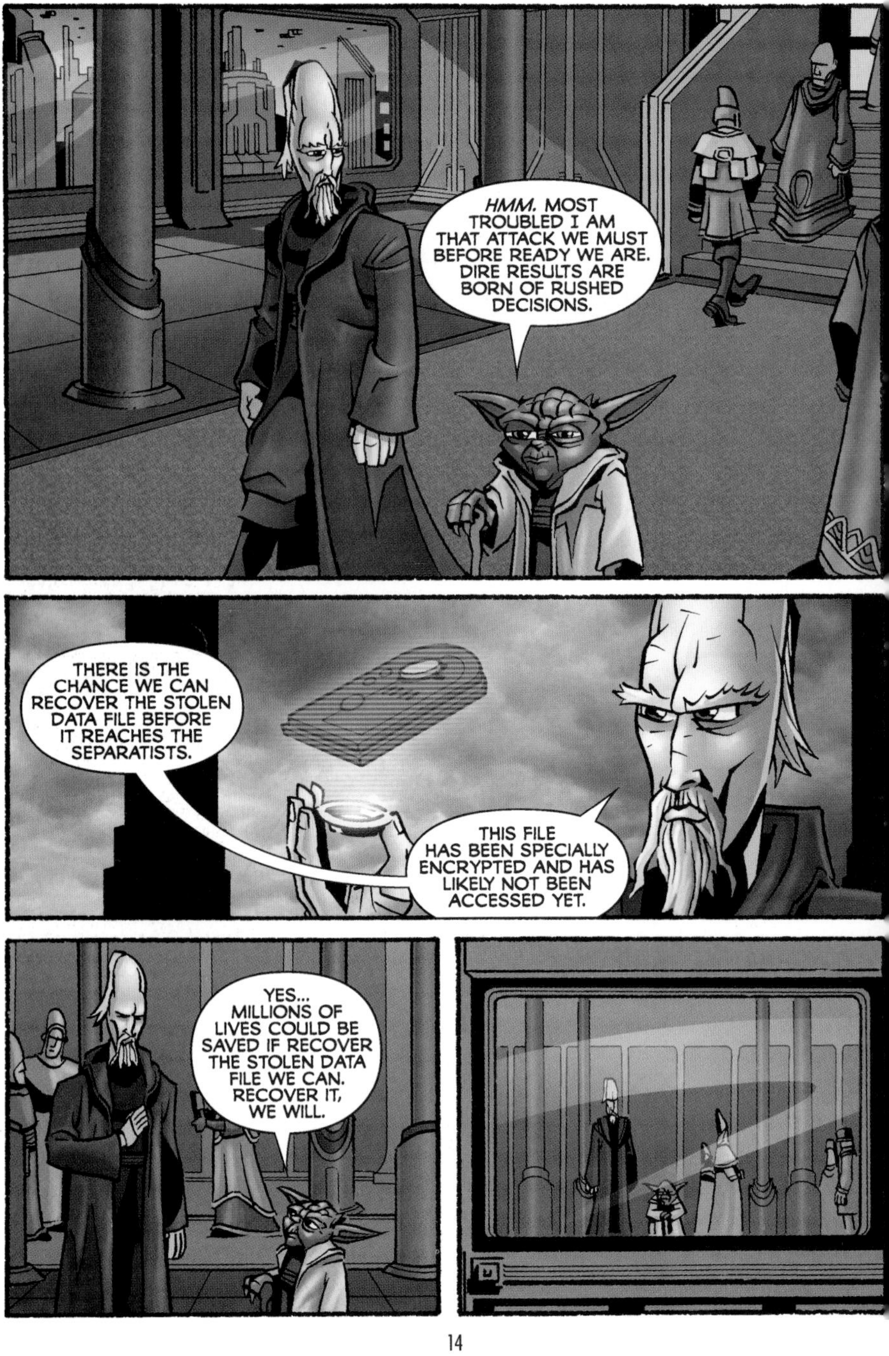
HMM. MOST TROUBLED I AM THAT ATTACK WE MUST BEFORE READY WE ARE. DIRE RESULTS ARE BORN OF RUSHED DECISIONS.
THERE IS THE CHANCE WE CAN RECOVER THE STOLEN DATA FILE BEFORE IT REACHES THE SEPARATISTS.
THIS FILE HAS BEEN SPECIALLY ENCRYPTED AND HAS LIKELY NOT BEEN ACCESSED YET.
YES... MILLIONS OF LIVES COULD BE SAVED IF RECOVER THE STOLEN DATA FILE WE CAN. RECOVER IT, WE WILL.

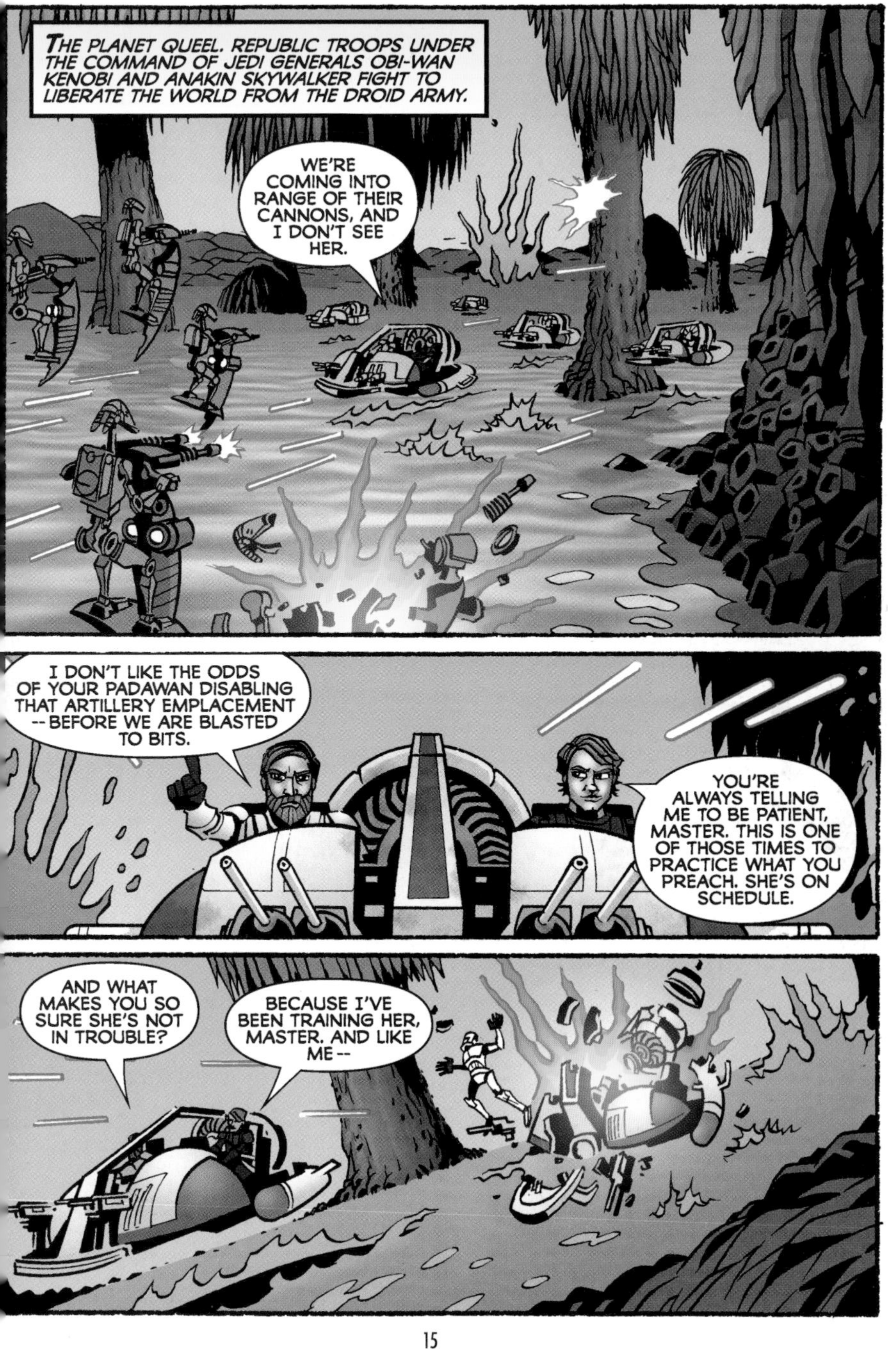
THE PLANET QUEEL. REPUBLIC TROOPS UNDER THE COMMAND OF JEDI GENERALS OBI-WAN KENOBI AND ANAKIN SKYWALKER FIGHT TO LIBERATE THE WORLD FROM THE DROID ARMY.
WE'RE COMING INTO RANGE OF THEIR CANNONS, AND I DON'T SEE HER.
I DON'T LIKE THE ODDS OF YOUR PADAWAN DISABLING THAT ARTILLERY EMPLACEMENT --BEFORE WE ARE BLASTED TO BITS.
YOU'RE ALWAYS TELLING ME TO BE PATIENT, MASTER. THIS IS ONE OF THOSE TIMES TO PRACTICE WHAT YOU PREACH. SHE'S ON SCHEDULE.
AND WHAT MAKES YOU SO SURE SHE'S NOT IN TROUBLE?
BECAUSE I'VE BEEN TRAINING HER, MASTER. AND LIKE ME --

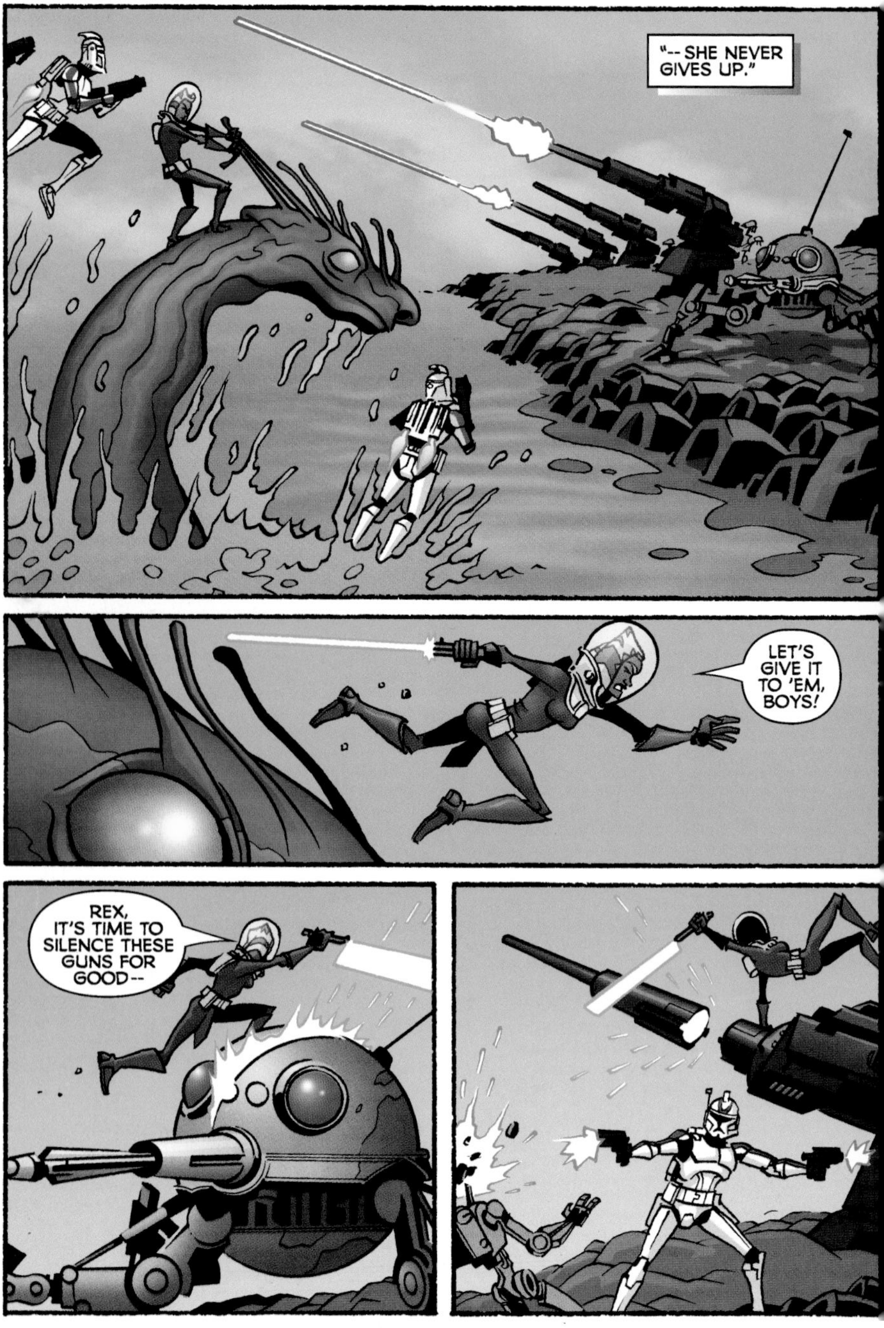
"-- SHE NEVER GIVES UP."
LET'S GIVE IT TO 'EM, BOYS!
REX, IT'S TIME TO SILENCE THESE GUNS FOR GOOD--

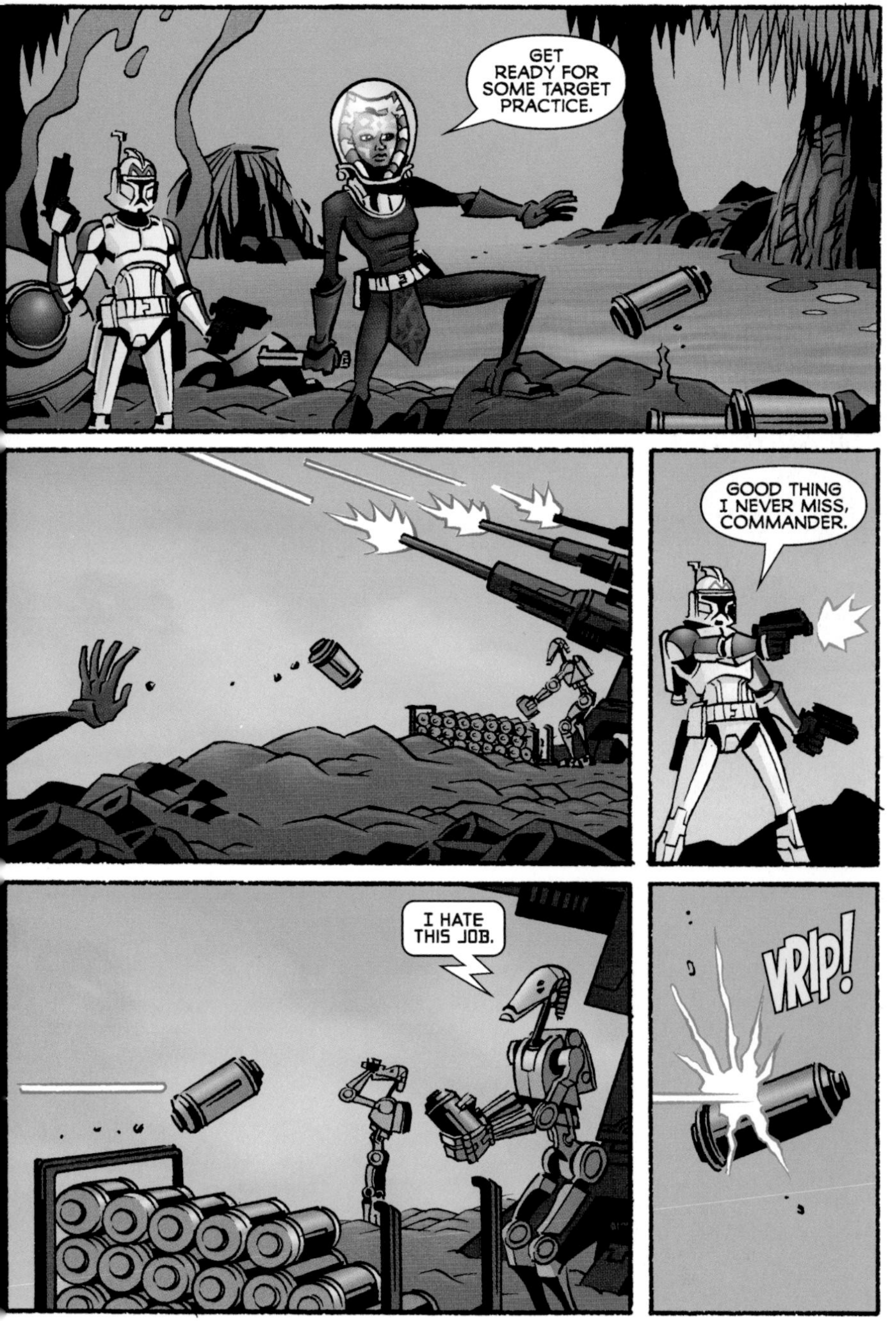
GET READY FOR SOME TARGET PRACTICE.
GOOD THING I NEVER MISS, COMMANDER.
I HATE THIS JOB.
VRIP!

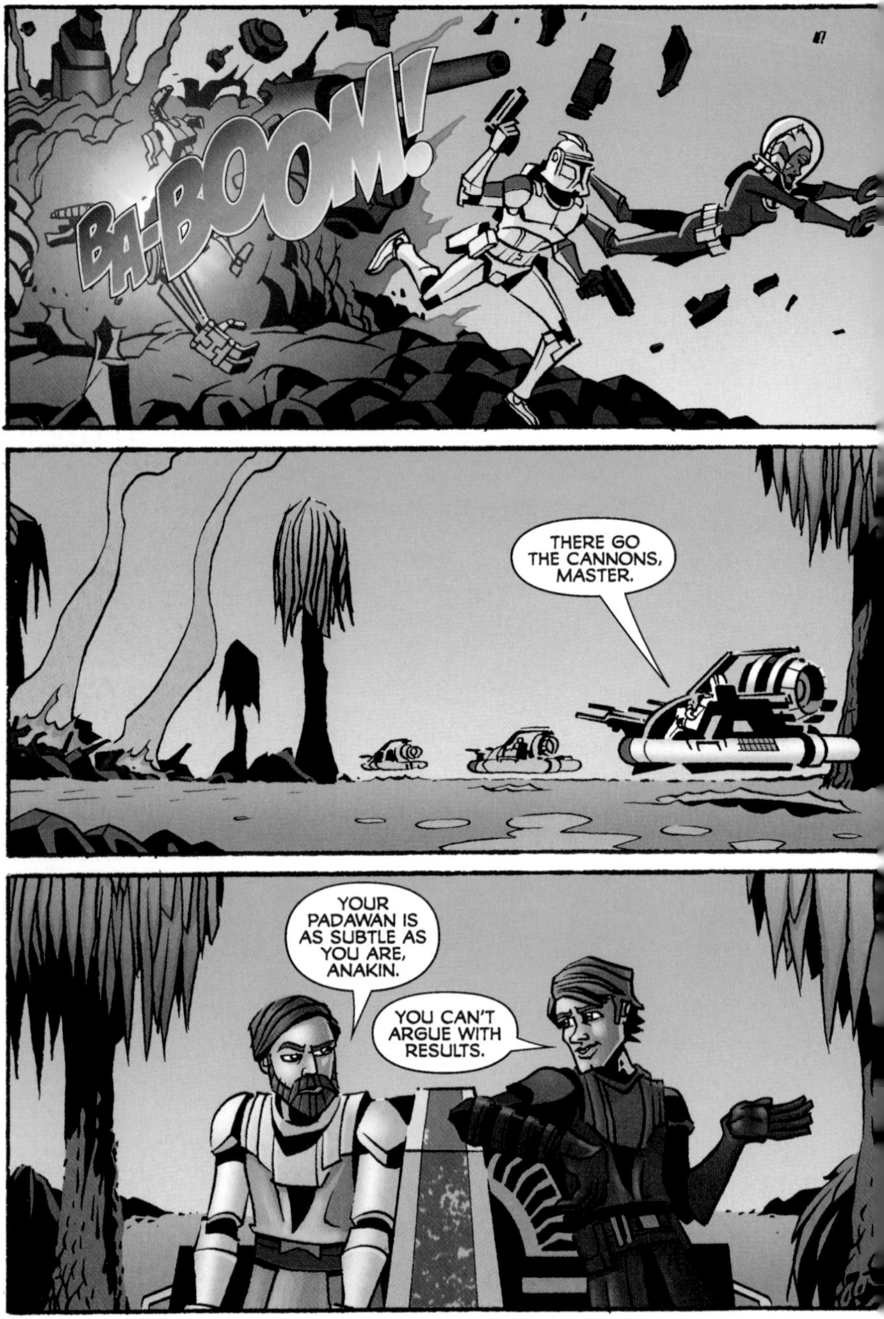
BA-BOOM!
THERE GO THE CANNONS, MASTER.
YOUR PADAWAN IS AS SUBTLE AS YOU ARE, ANAKIN.
YOU CAN'T ARGUE WITH RESULTS.

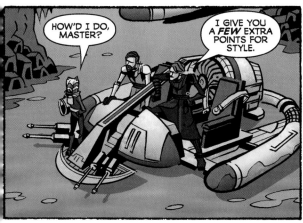

HOW'D I DO, MASTER?

I GIVE YOU A *FEW* EXTRA POINTS FOR STYLE.

A FEW? I DESERVE *A LOT.*

YOU DID WELL CLEARING THE PATH FOR OUR ASSAULT ON THE DROID COMMAND BASE -- BUT NOW THEY KNOW WE'RE COMING.

RIGHT. SORRY, MASTER OBI-WAN.

NEXT TIME, I'LL TRY TO DESTROY AN ENTIRE DROID ARTILLERY BATTERY A LITTLE QUIETER.

GENERAL KENOBI, THERE'S AN URGENT MESSAGE FOR YOU AND SKYWALKER FROM THE JEDI TEMPLE...

ACKNOWLEDGED, CODY.

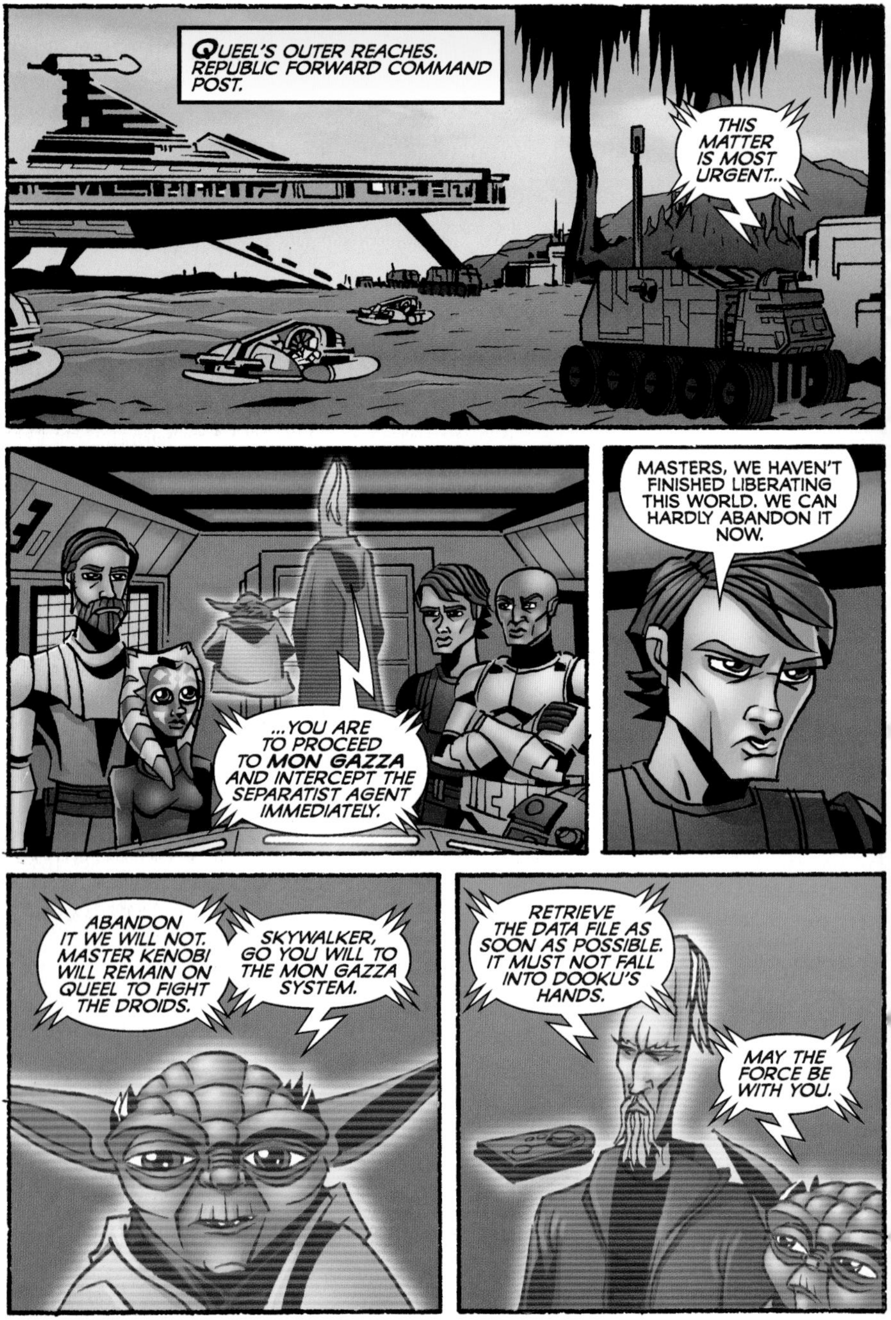
QUEEL'S OUTER REACHES. REPUBLIC FORWARD COMMAND POST.
THIS MATTER IS MOST URGENT...
...YOU ARE TO PROCEED TO MON GAZZA AND INTERCEPT THE SEPARATIST AGENT IMMEDIATELY.
MASTERS, WE HAVEN'T FINISHED LIBERATING THIS WORLD. WE CAN HARDLY ABANDON IT NOW.
ABANDON IT WE WILL NOT. MASTER KENOBI WILL REMAIN ON QUEEL TO FIGHT THE DROIDS.
SKYWALKER, GO YOU WILL TO THE MON GAZZA SYSTEM.
RETRIEVE THE DATA FILE AS SOON AS POSSIBLE. IT MUST NOT FALL INTO DOOKU'S HANDS.
MAY THE FORCE BE WITH YOU.

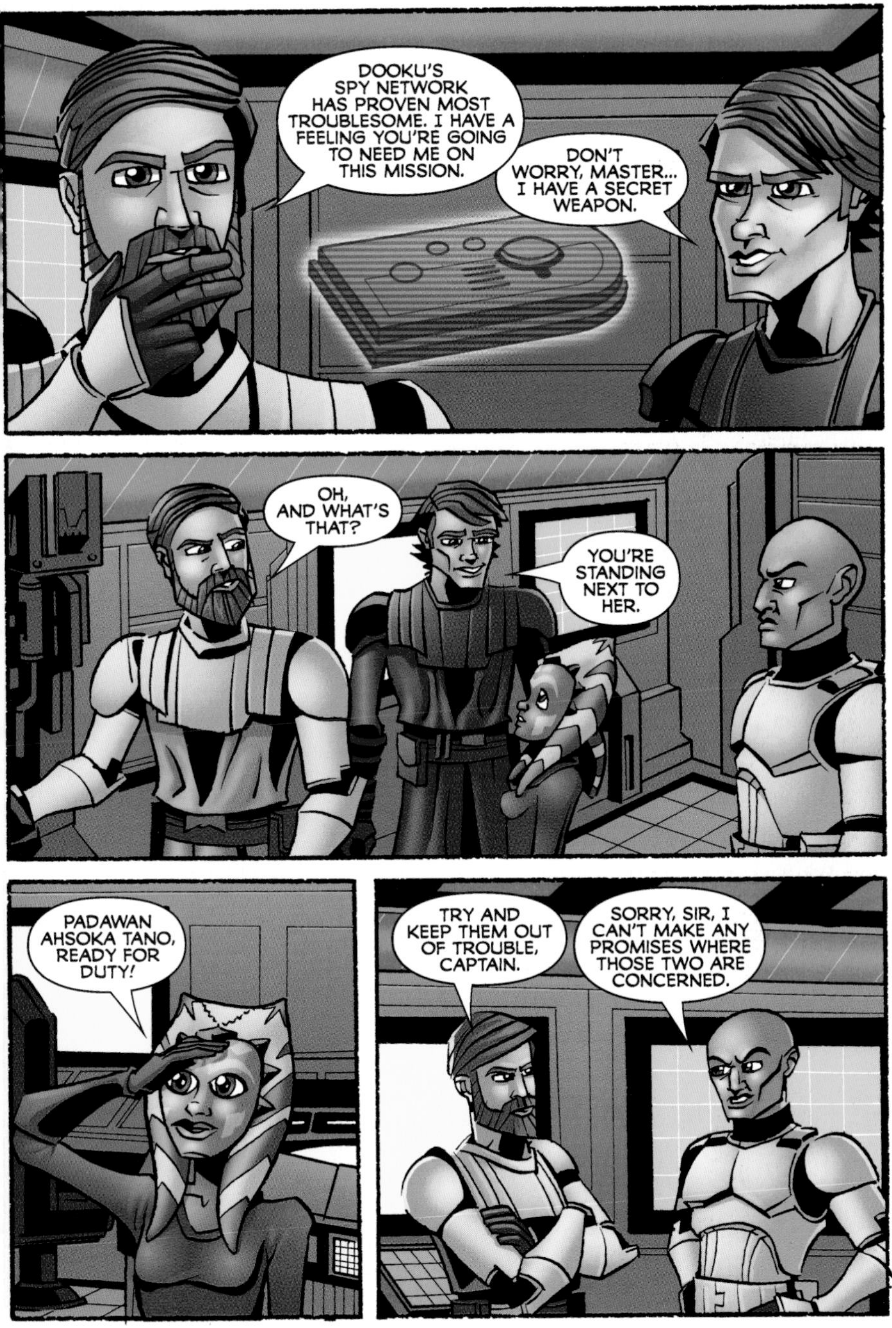
DOOKU'S SPY NETWORK HAS PROVEN MOST TROUBLESOME. I HAVE A FEELING YOU'RE GOING TO NEED ME ON THIS MISSION.
DON'T WORRY, MASTER... I HAVE A SECRET WEAPON.
OH, AND WHAT'S THAT?
YOU'RE STANDING NEXT TO HER.
PADAWAN AHSOKA TANO, READY FOR DUTY!
TRY AND KEEP THEM OUT OF TROUBLE, CAPTAIN.
SORRY, SIR, I CAN'T MAKE ANY PROMISES WHERE THOSE TWO ARE CONCERNED.

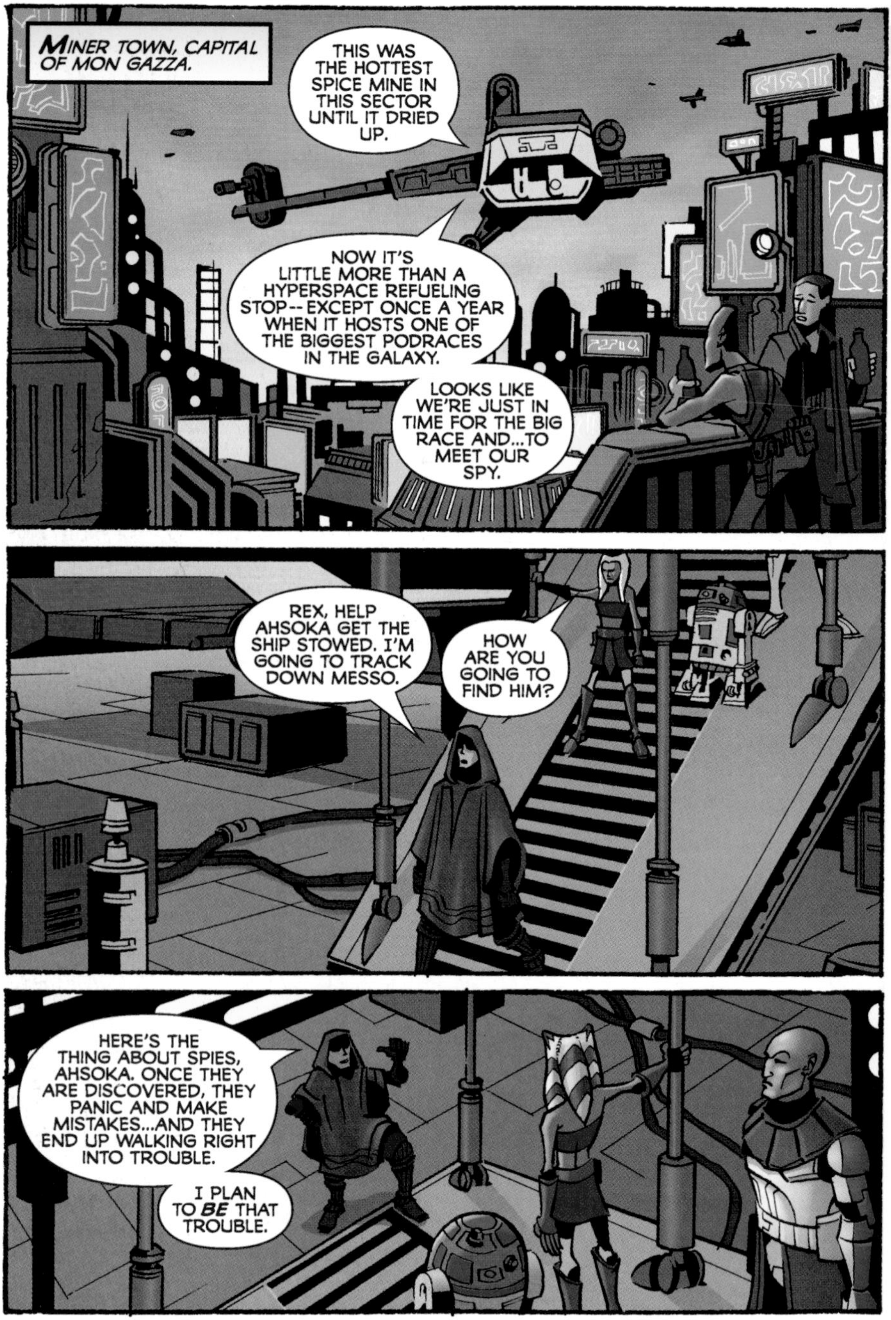
MINER TOWN, CAPITAL OF MON GAZZA.
THIS WAS THE HOTTEST SPICE MINE IN THIS SECTOR UNTIL IT DRIED UP.
NOW IT'S LITTLE MORE THAN A HYPERSPACE REFUELING STOP-- EXCEPT ONCE A YEAR WHEN IT HOSTS ONE OF THE BIGGEST PODRACES IN THE GALAXY.
LOOKS LIKE WE'RE JUST IN TIME FOR THE BIG RACE AND...TO MEET OUR SPY.
REX, HELP AHSOKA GET THE SHIP STOWED. I'M GOING TO TRACK DOWN MESSO.
HOW ARE YOU GOING TO FIND HIM?
HERE'S THE THING ABOUT SPIES, AHSOKA. ONCE THEY ARE DISCOVERED, THEY PANIC AND MAKE MISTAKES...AND THEY END UP WALKING RIGHT INTO TROUBLE.
I PLAN TO *BE* THAT TROUBLE.

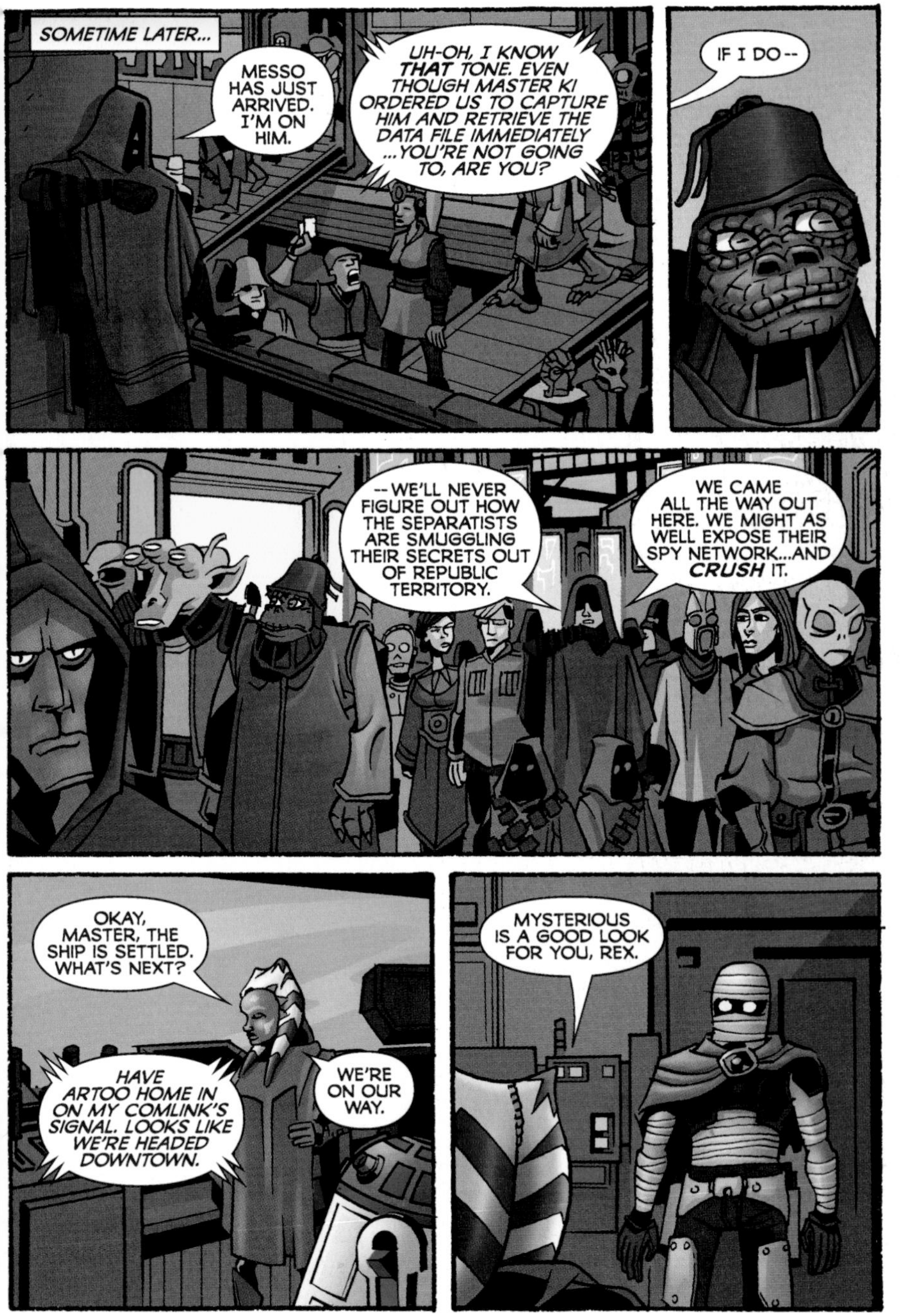
SOMETIME LATER...
MESSO HAS JUST ARRIVED. I'M ON HIM.
UH-OH, I KNOW **THAT** TONE. EVEN THOUGH MASTER KI ORDERED US TO CAPTURE HIM AND RETRIEVE THE DATA FILE IMMEDIATELY ...YOU'RE NOT GOING TO, ARE YOU?
IF I DO --
-- WE'LL NEVER FIGURE OUT HOW THE SEPARATISTS ARE SMUGGLING THEIR SECRETS OUT OF REPUBLIC TERRITORY.
WE CAME ALL THE WAY OUT HERE. WE MIGHT AS WELL EXPOSE THEIR SPY NETWORK...AND ***CRUSH*** IT.
OKAY, MASTER, THE SHIP IS SETTLED. WHAT'S NEXT?
HAVE ARTOO HOME IN ON MY COMLINK'S SIGNAL. LOOKS LIKE WE'RE HEADED DOWNTOWN.
WE'RE ON OUR WAY.
MYSTERIOUS IS A GOOD LOOK FOR YOU, REX.

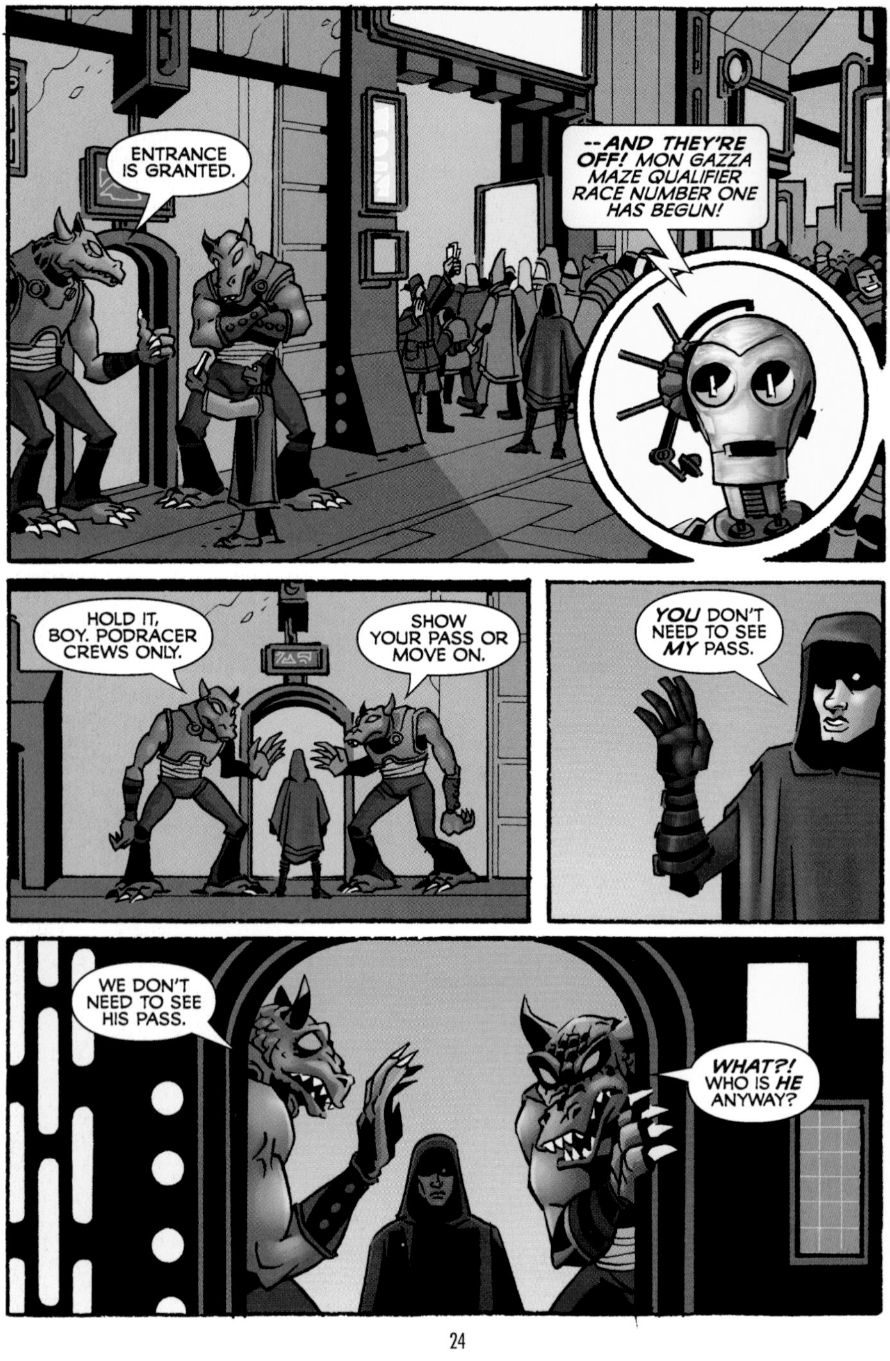
ENTRANCE IS GRANTED.
--AND THEY'RE OFF! MON GAZZA MAZE QUALIFIER RACE NUMBER ONE HAS BEGUN!
HOLD IT, BOY. PODRACER CREWS ONLY.
SHOW YOUR PASS OR MOVE ON.
YOU DON'T NEED TO SEE MY PASS.
WE DON'T NEED TO SEE HIS PASS.
WHAT?! WHO IS HE ANYWAY?

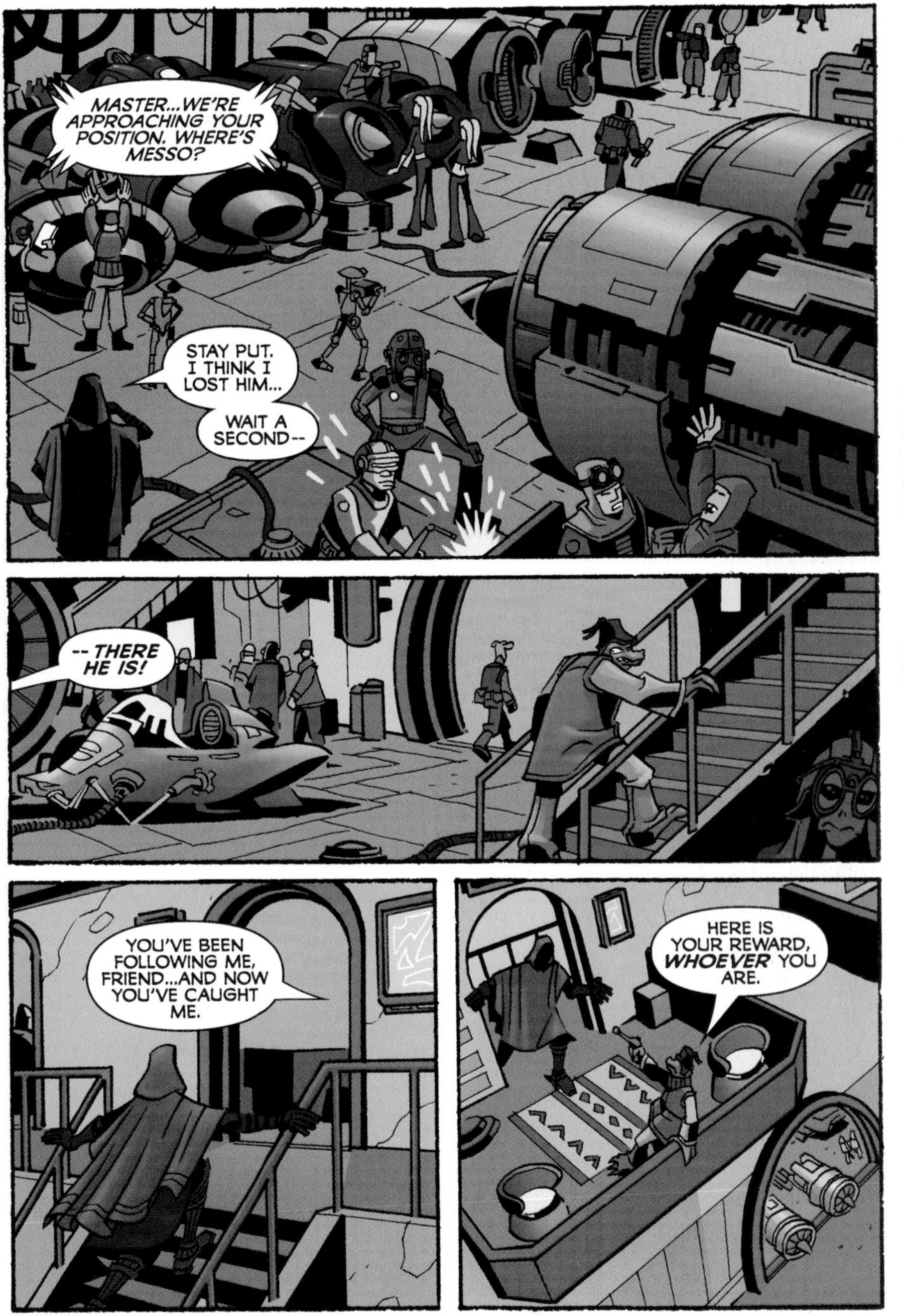
MASTER...WE'RE APPROACHING YOUR POSITION. WHERE'S MESSO?
STAY PUT. I THINK I LOST HIM...
WAIT A SECOND--
--THERE HE IS!
YOU'VE BEEN FOLLOWING ME, FRIEND...AND NOW YOU'VE CAUGHT ME.
HERE IS YOUR REWARD, *WHOEVER* YOU ARE.

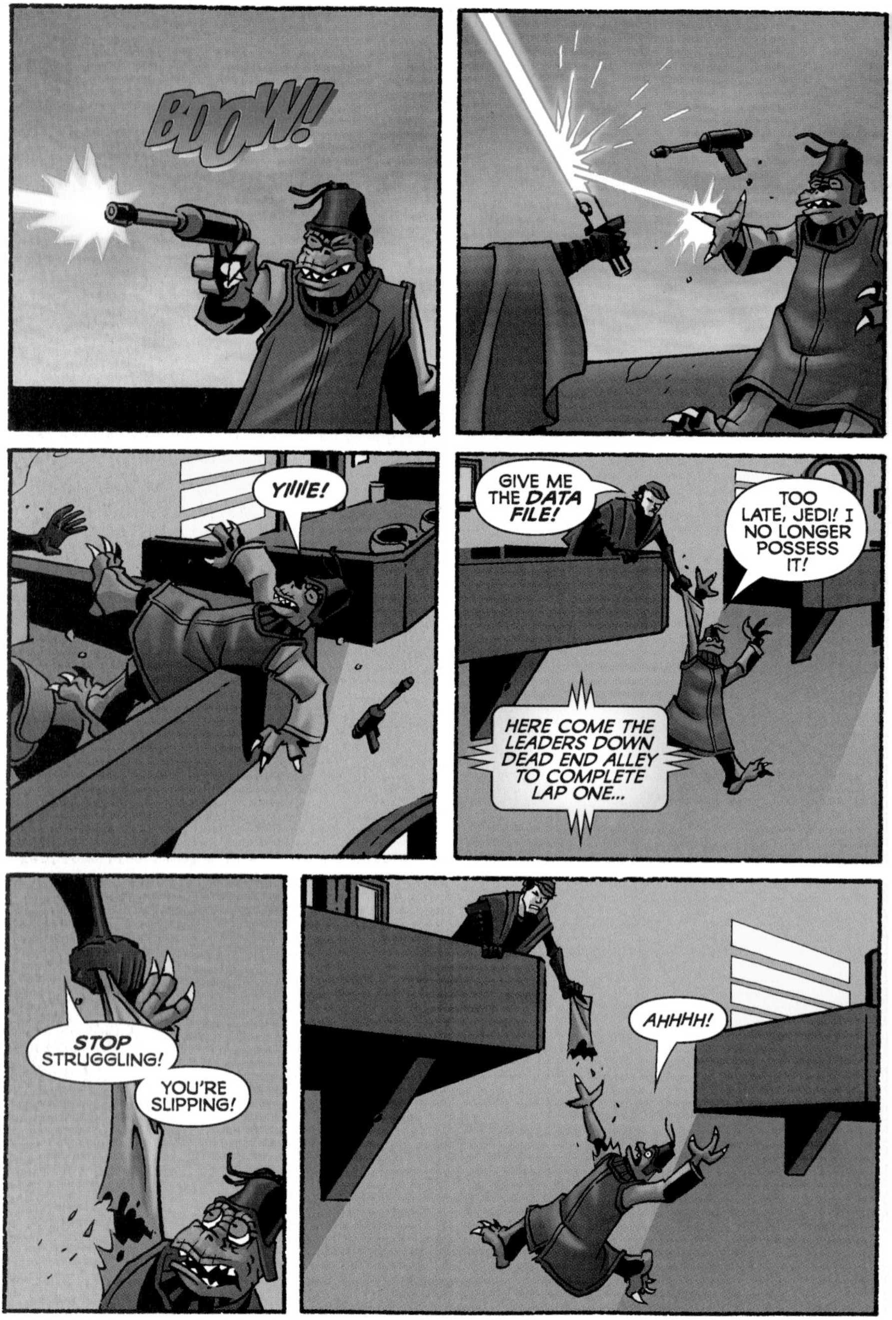
BOOM!
YIIIIE!
GIVE ME THE DATA FILE!
TOO LATE, JEDI! I NO LONGER POSSESS IT!
HERE COME THE LEADERS DOWN DEAD END ALLEY TO COMPLETE LAP ONE...
STOP STRUGGLING!
YOU'RE SLIPPING!
AHHHH!

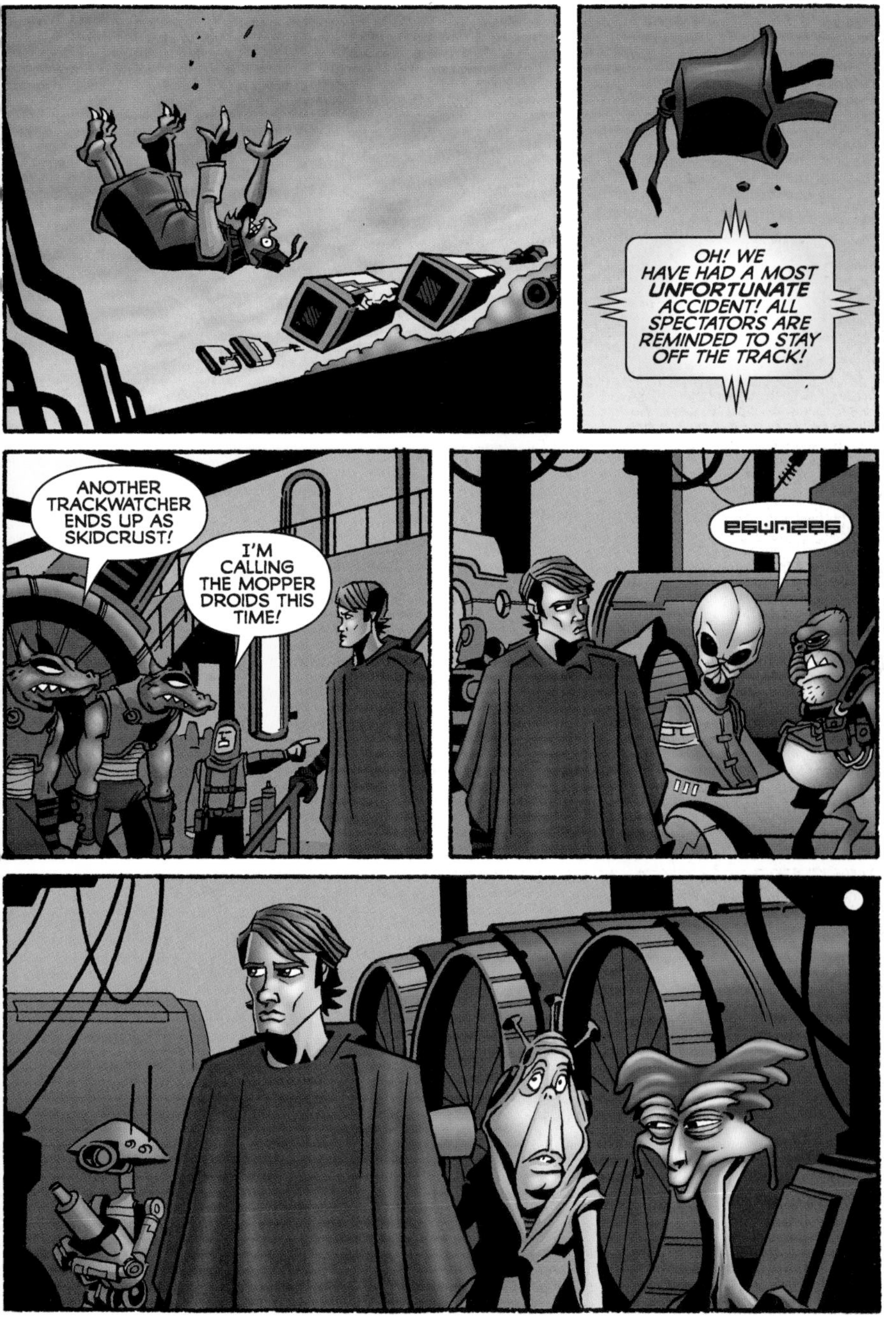
OH! WE HAVE HAD A MOST **UNFORTUNATE** ACCIDENT! ALL SPECTATORS ARE REMINDED TO STAY OFF THE TRACK!
ANOTHER TRACKWATCHER ENDS UP AS SKIDCRUST!
I'M CALLING THE MOPPER DROIDS THIS TIME!

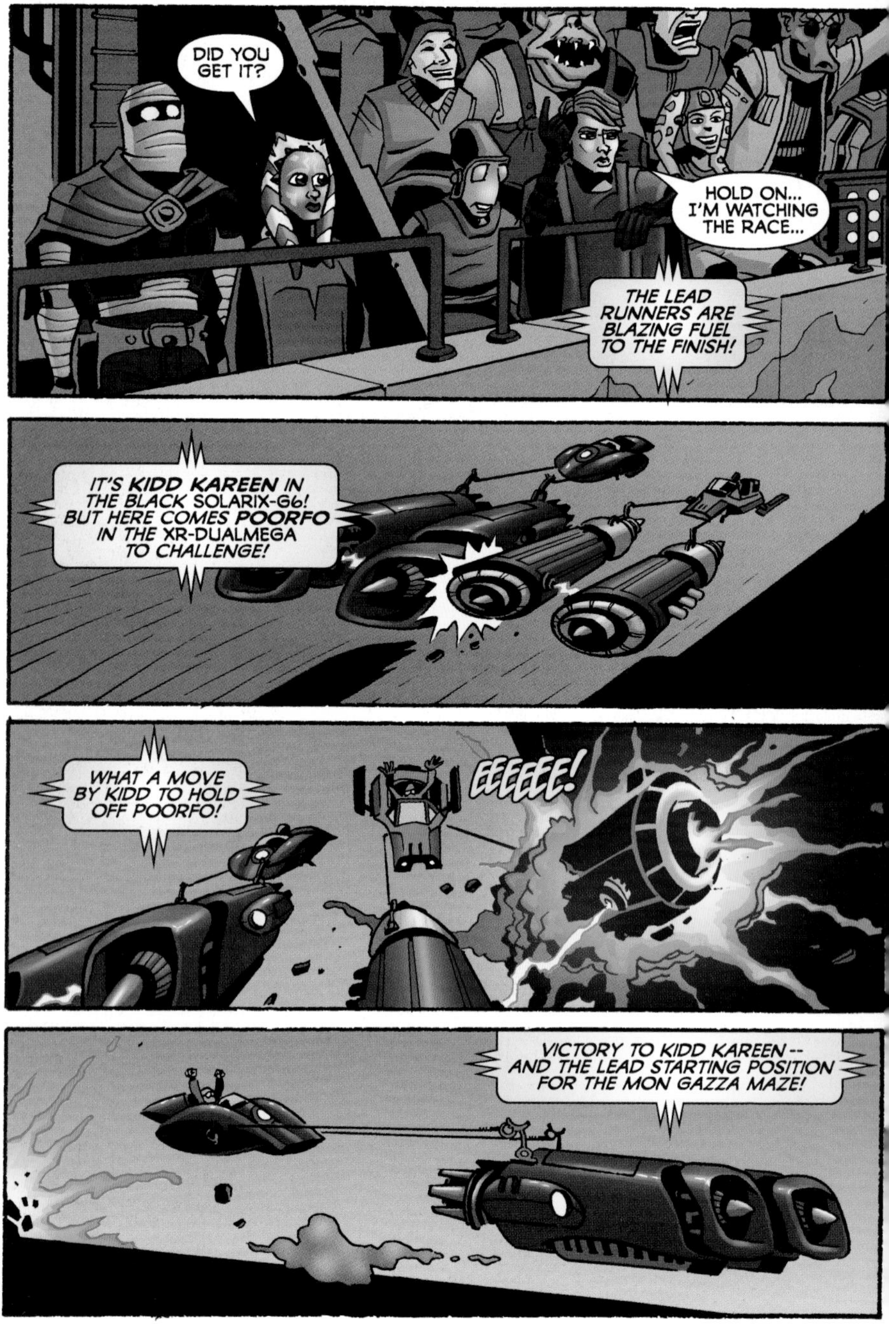
DID YOU GET IT?
HOLD ON... I'M WATCHING THE RACE...
THE LEAD RUNNERS ARE BLAZING FUEL TO THE FINISH!
IT'S KIDD KAREEN IN THE BLACK SOLARIX-G6! BUT HERE COMES POORFO IN THE XR-DUALMEGA TO CHALLENGE!
WHAT A MOVE BY KIDD TO HOLD OFF POORFO!
EEEEEE!
VICTORY TO KIDD KAREEN -- AND THE LEAD STARTING POSITION FOR THE MON GAZZA MAZE!

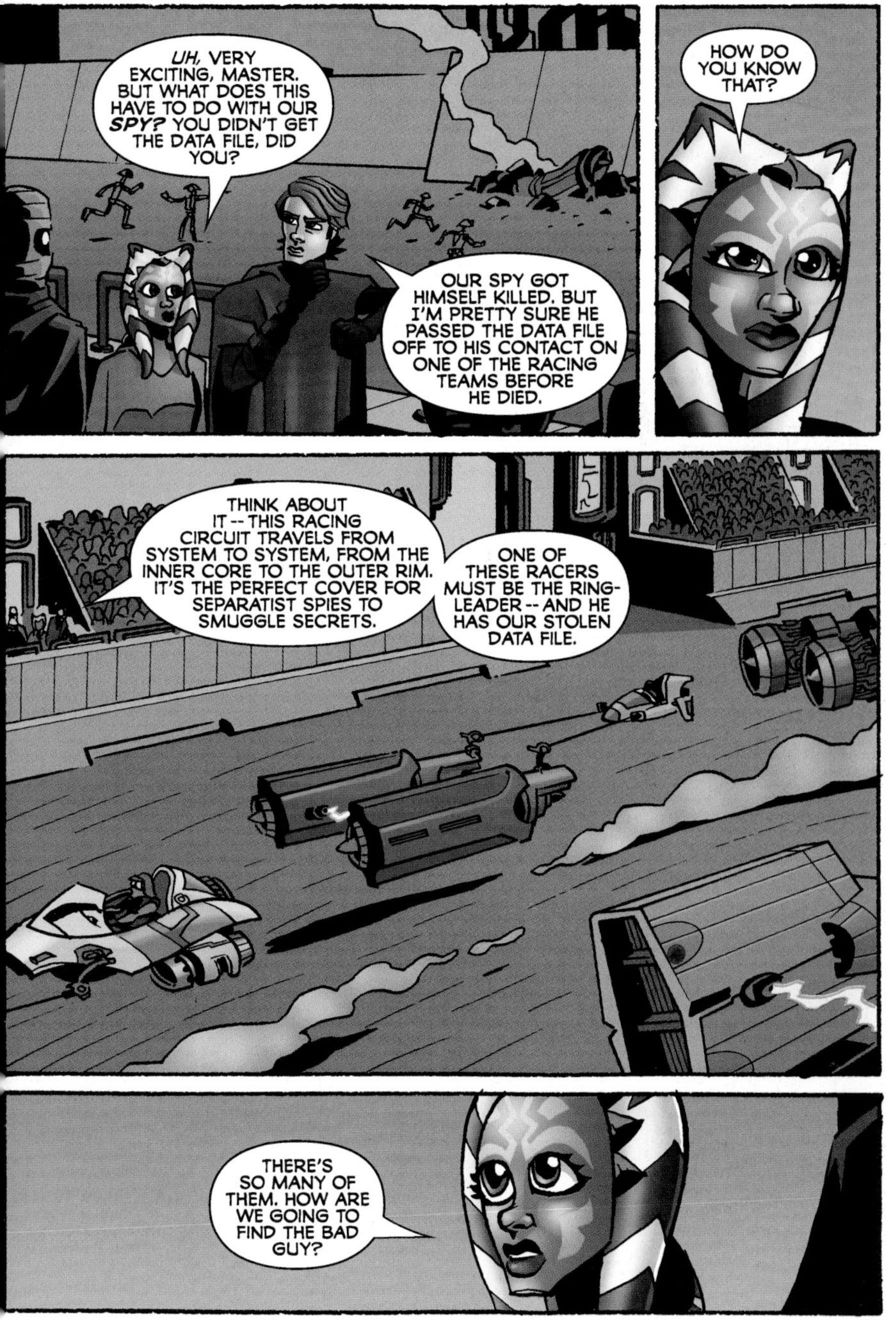
UH, VERY EXCITING, MASTER. BUT WHAT DOES THIS HAVE TO DO WITH OUR SPY? YOU DIDN'T GET THE DATA FILE, DID YOU?
OUR SPY GOT HIMSELF KILLED. BUT I'M PRETTY SURE HE PASSED THE DATA FILE OFF TO HIS CONTACT ON ONE OF THE RACING TEAMS BEFORE HE DIED.
HOW DO YOU KNOW THAT?
THINK ABOUT IT -- THIS RACING CIRCUIT TRAVELS FROM SYSTEM TO SYSTEM, FROM THE INNER CORE TO THE OUTER RIM. IT'S THE PERFECT COVER FOR SEPARATIST SPIES TO SMUGGLE SECRETS.
ONE OF THESE RACERS MUST BE THE RING-LEADER -- AND HE HAS OUR STOLEN DATA FILE.
THERE'S SO MANY OF THEM. HOW ARE WE GOING TO FIND THE BAD GUY?

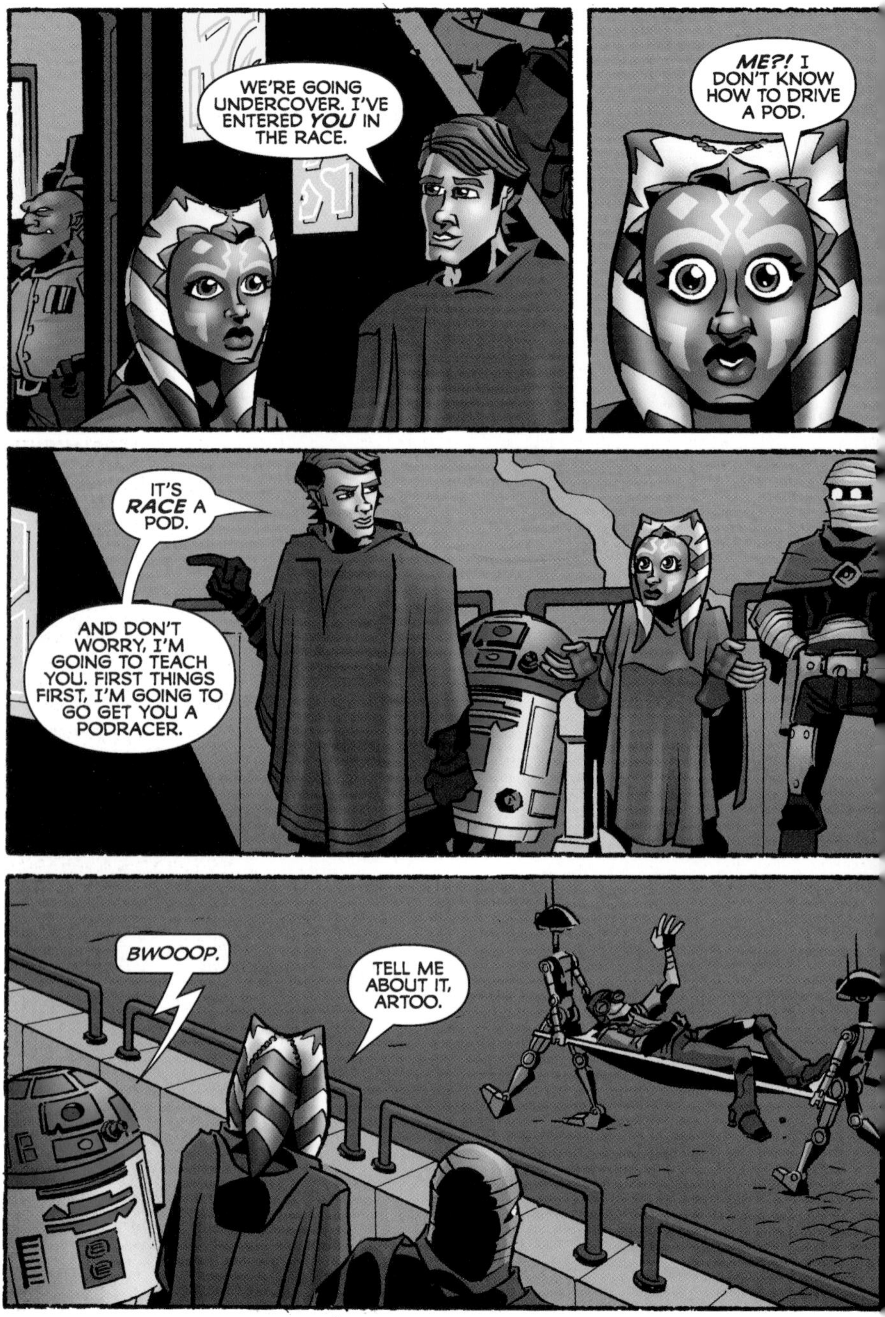
WE'RE GOING UNDERCOVER. I'VE ENTERED *YOU* IN THE RACE.
ME?! I DON'T KNOW HOW TO DRIVE A POD.
IT'S *RACE* A POD.
AND DON'T WORRY, I'M GOING TO TEACH YOU. FIRST THINGS FIRST, I'M GOING TO GO GET YOU A PODRACER.
BWOOOP.
TELL ME ABOUT IT, ARTOO.

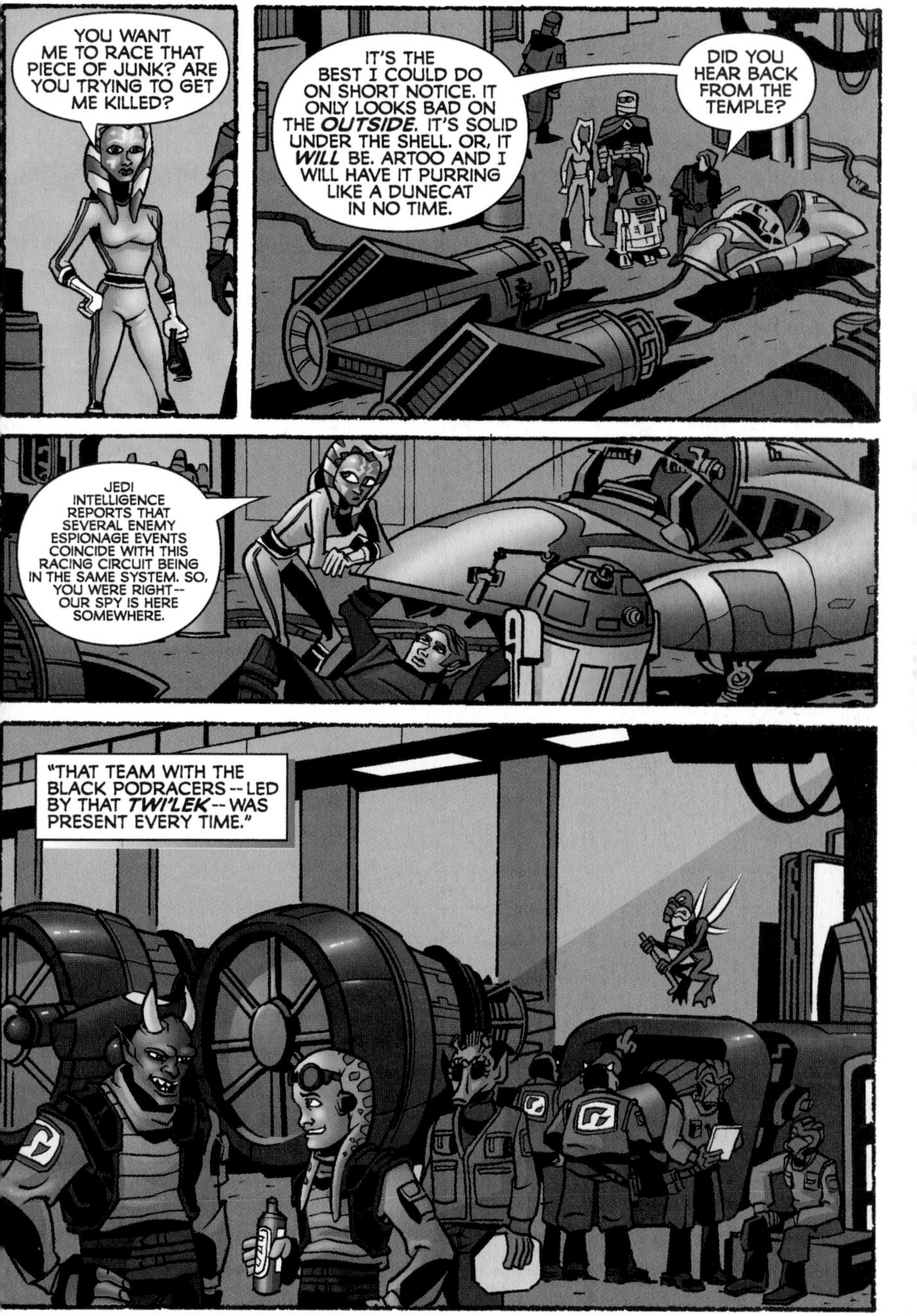

YOU WANT ME TO RACE THAT PIECE OF JUNK? ARE YOU TRYING TO GET ME KILLED?
IT'S THE BEST I COULD DO ON SHORT NOTICE. IT ONLY LOOKS BAD ON THE *OUTSIDE*. IT'S SOLID UNDER THE SHELL. OR, IT *WILL* BE. ARTOO AND I WILL HAVE IT PURRING LIKE A DUNECAT IN NO TIME.
DID YOU HEAR BACK FROM THE TEMPLE?
JEDI INTELLIGENCE REPORTS THAT SEVERAL ENEMY ESPIONAGE EVENTS COINCIDE WITH THIS RACING CIRCUIT BEING IN THE SAME SYSTEM. SO, YOU WERE RIGHT-- OUR SPY IS HERE SOMEWHERE.
"THAT TEAM WITH THE BLACK PODRACERS--LED BY THAT *TWI'LEK*--WAS PRESENT EVERY TIME."

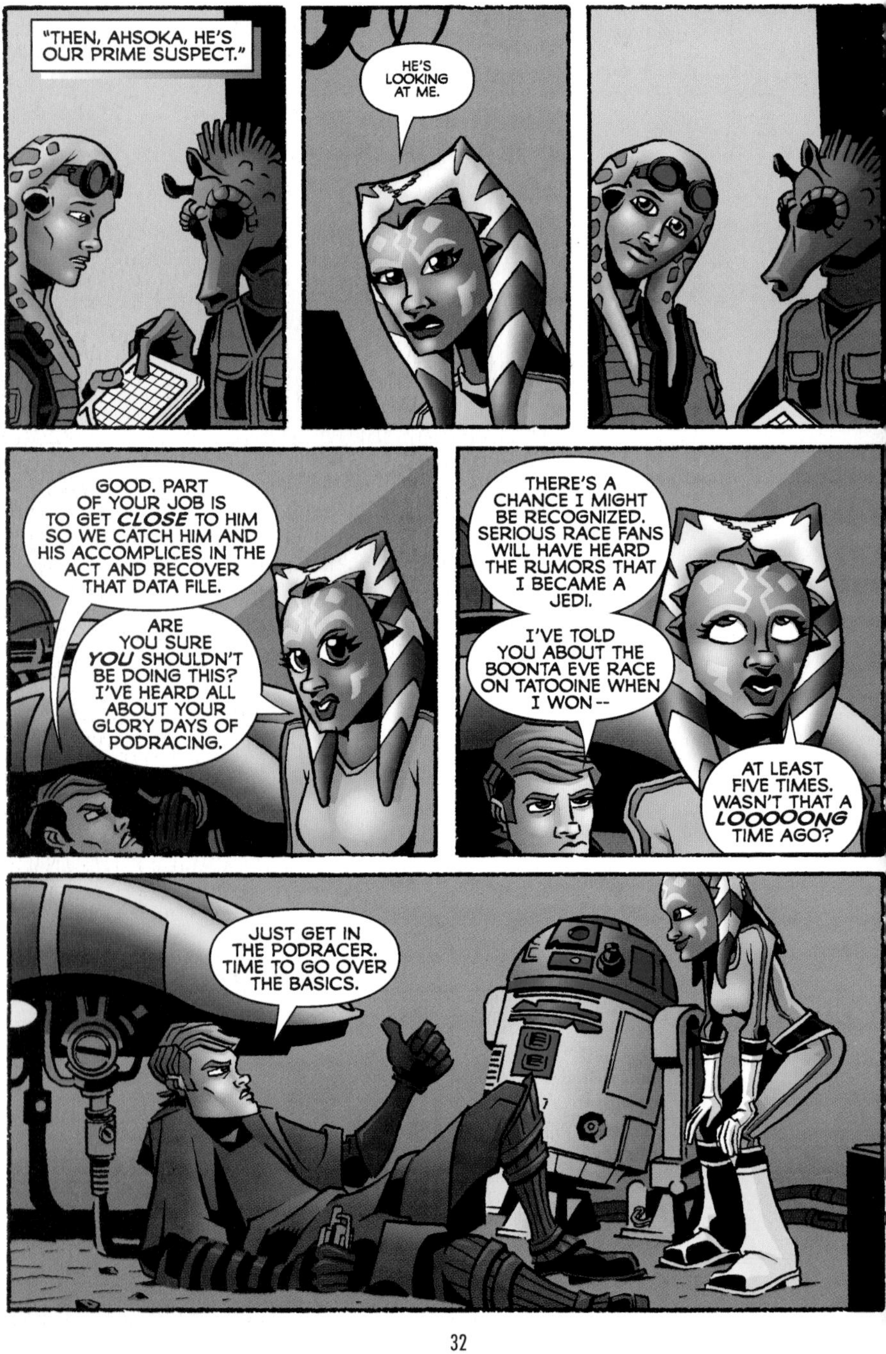
"THEN, AHSOKA, HE'S OUR PRIME SUSPECT."
HE'S LOOKING AT ME.
GOOD. PART OF YOUR JOB IS TO GET *CLOSE* TO HIM SO WE CATCH HIM AND HIS ACCOMPLICES IN THE ACT AND RECOVER THAT DATA FILE.
ARE YOU SURE *YOU* SHOULDN'T BE DOING THIS? I'VE HEARD ALL ABOUT YOUR GLORY DAYS OF PODRACING.
THERE'S A CHANCE I MIGHT BE RECOGNIZED. SERIOUS RACE FANS WILL HAVE HEARD THE RUMORS THAT I BECAME A JEDI.
I'VE TOLD YOU ABOUT THE BOONTA EVE RACE ON TATOOINE WHEN I WON--
AT LEAST FIVE TIMES. WASN'T THAT A *LOOOOONG* TIME AGO?
JUST GET IN THE PODRACER. TIME TO GO OVER THE BASICS.

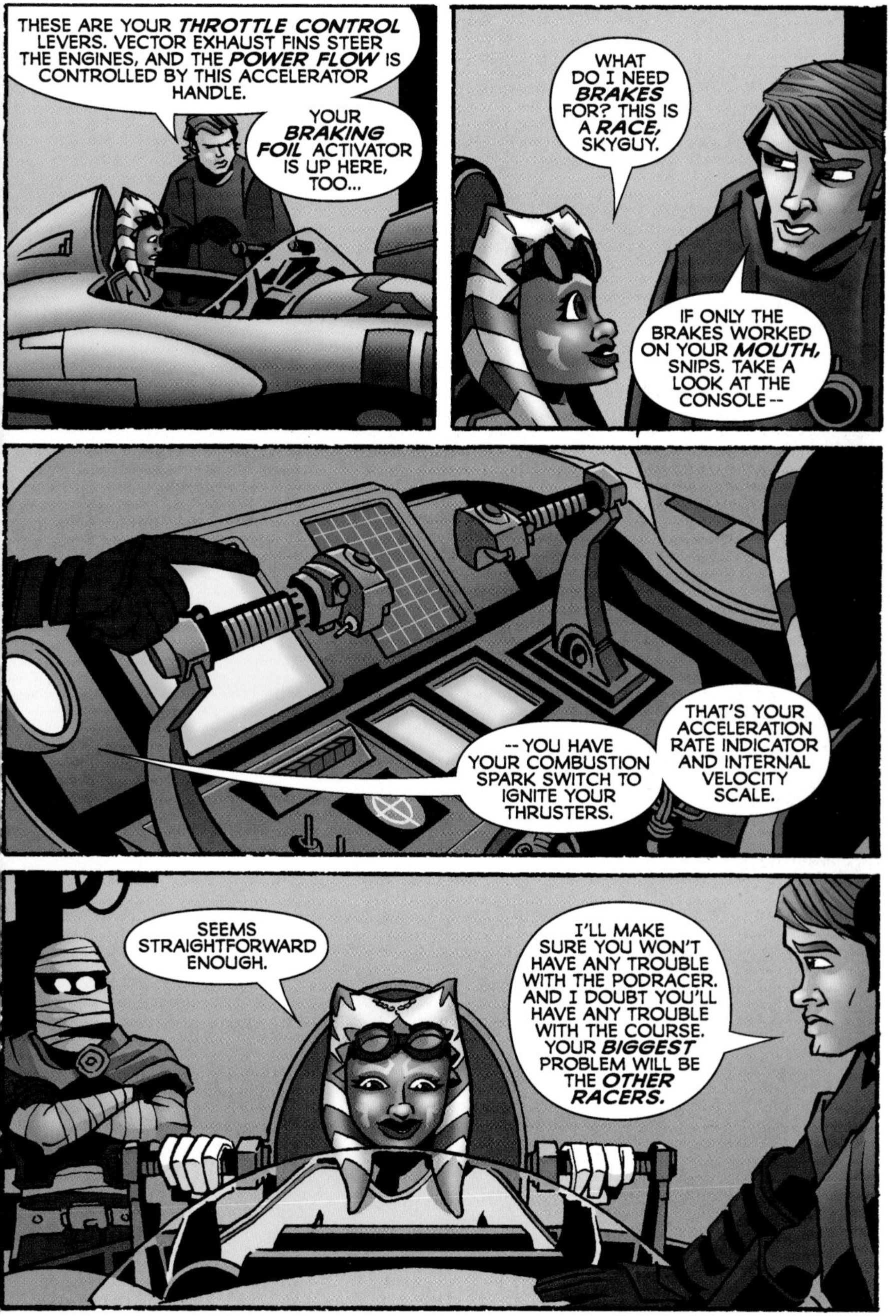
THESE ARE YOUR THROTTLE CONTROL LEVERS. VECTOR EXHAUST FINS STEER THE ENGINES, AND THE POWER FLOW IS CONTROLLED BY THIS ACCELERATOR HANDLE.
YOUR BRAKING FOIL ACTIVATOR IS UP HERE, TOO...
WHAT DO I NEED BRAKES FOR? THIS IS A RACE, SKYGUY.
IF ONLY THE BRAKES WORKED ON YOUR MOUTH, SNIPS. TAKE A LOOK AT THE CONSOLE --
THAT'S YOUR ACCELERATION RATE INDICATOR AND INTERNAL VELOCITY SCALE.
-- YOU HAVE YOUR COMBUSTION SPARK SWITCH TO IGNITE YOUR THRUSTERS.
SEEMS STRAIGHTFORWARD ENOUGH.
I'LL MAKE SURE YOU WON'T HAVE ANY TROUBLE WITH THE PODRACER. AND I DOUBT YOU'LL HAVE ANY TROUBLE WITH THE COURSE. YOUR BIGGEST PROBLEM WILL BE THE OTHER RACERS.

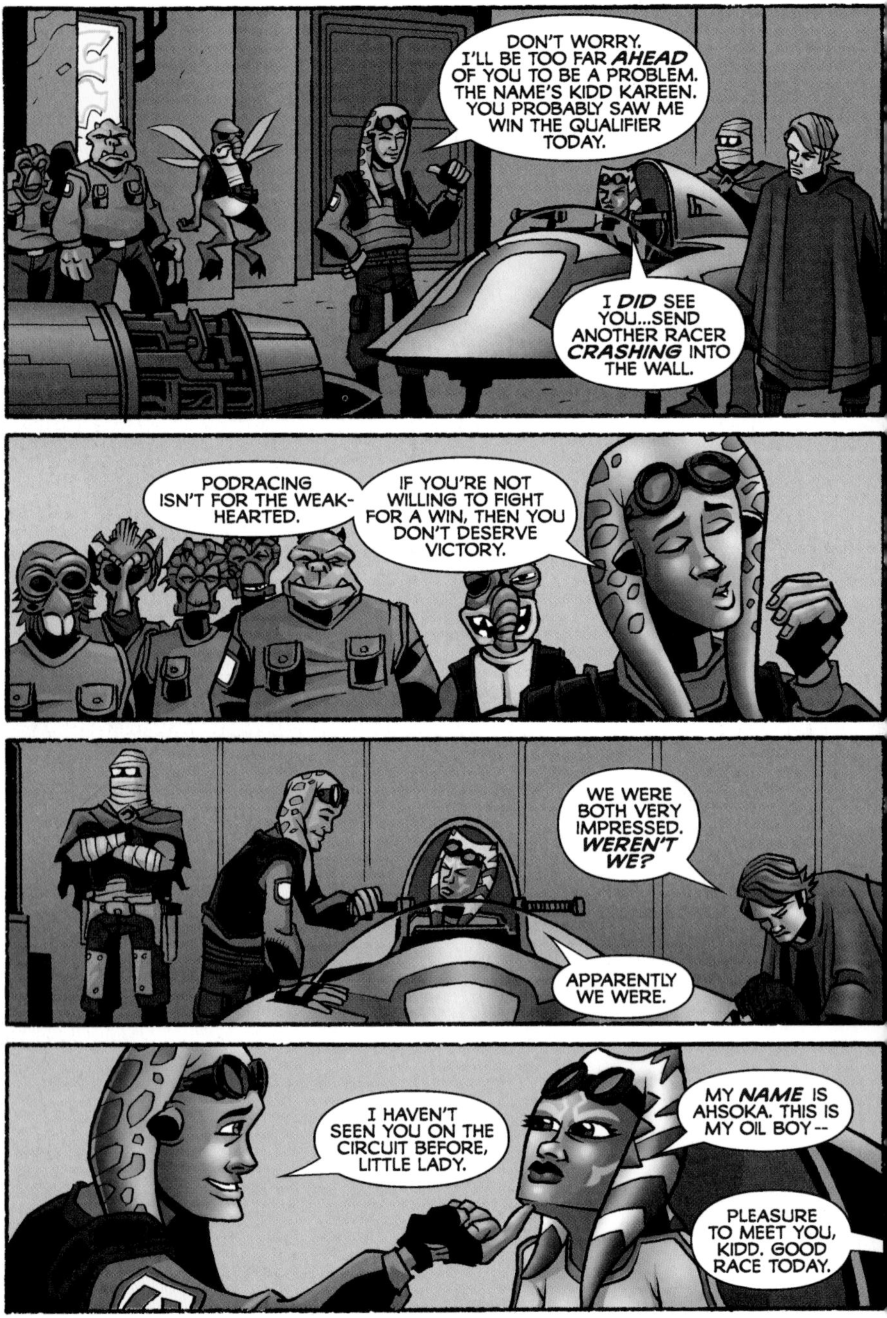
DON'T WORRY. I'LL BE TOO FAR AHEAD OF YOU TO BE A PROBLEM. THE NAME'S KIDD KAREEN. YOU PROBABLY SAW ME WIN THE QUALIFIER TODAY.
I DID SEE YOU...SEND ANOTHER RACER CRASHING INTO THE WALL.
PODRACING ISN'T FOR THE WEAK-HEARTED.
IF YOU'RE NOT WILLING TO FIGHT FOR A WIN, THEN YOU DON'T DESERVE VICTORY.
WE WERE BOTH VERY IMPRESSED. WEREN'T WE?
APPARENTLY WE WERE.
I HAVEN'T SEEN YOU ON THE CIRCUIT BEFORE, LITTLE LADY.
MY NAME IS AHSOKA. THIS IS MY OIL BOY--
PLEASURE TO MEET YOU, KIDD. GOOD RACE TODAY.

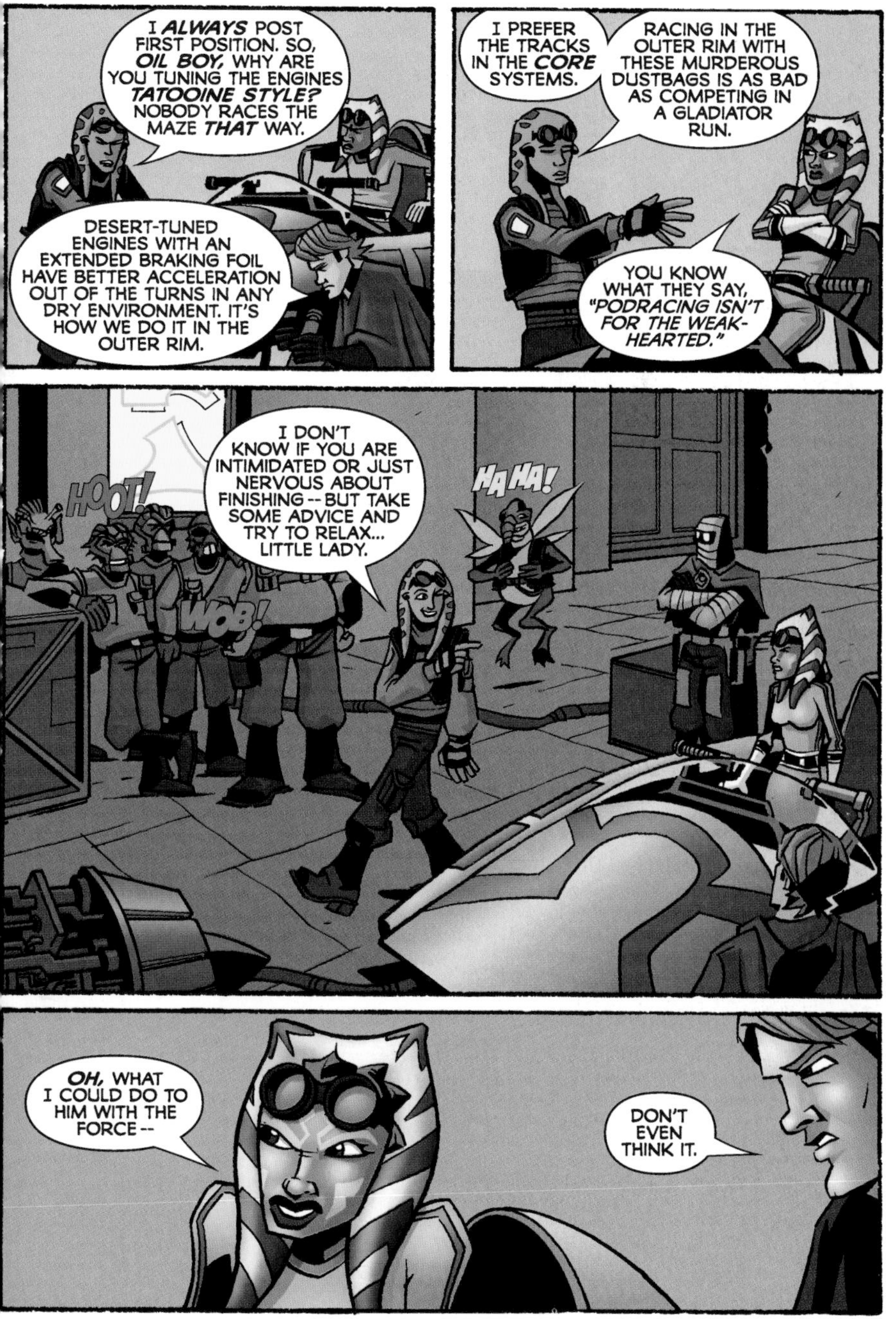
I *ALWAYS* POST FIRST POSITION. SO, *OIL BOY,* WHY ARE YOU TUNING THE ENGINES *TATOOINE STYLE?* NOBODY RACES THE MAZE *THAT* WAY.
DESERT-TUNED ENGINES WITH AN EXTENDED BRAKING FOIL HAVE BETTER ACCELERATION OUT OF THE TURNS IN ANY DRY ENVIRONMENT. IT'S HOW WE DO IT IN THE OUTER RIM.
I PREFER THE TRACKS IN THE *CORE* SYSTEMS.
RACING IN THE OUTER RIM WITH THESE MURDEROUS DUSTBAGS IS AS BAD AS COMPETING IN A GLADIATOR RUN.
YOU KNOW WHAT THEY SAY, *"PODRACING ISN'T FOR THE WEAK-HEARTED."*
HOOT!
I DON'T KNOW IF YOU ARE INTIMIDATED OR JUST NERVOUS ABOUT FINISHING -- BUT TAKE SOME ADVICE AND TRY TO RELAX... LITTLE LADY.
HA HA!
WOB!
OH, WHAT I COULD DO TO HIM WITH THE FORCE --
DON'T EVEN THINK IT.

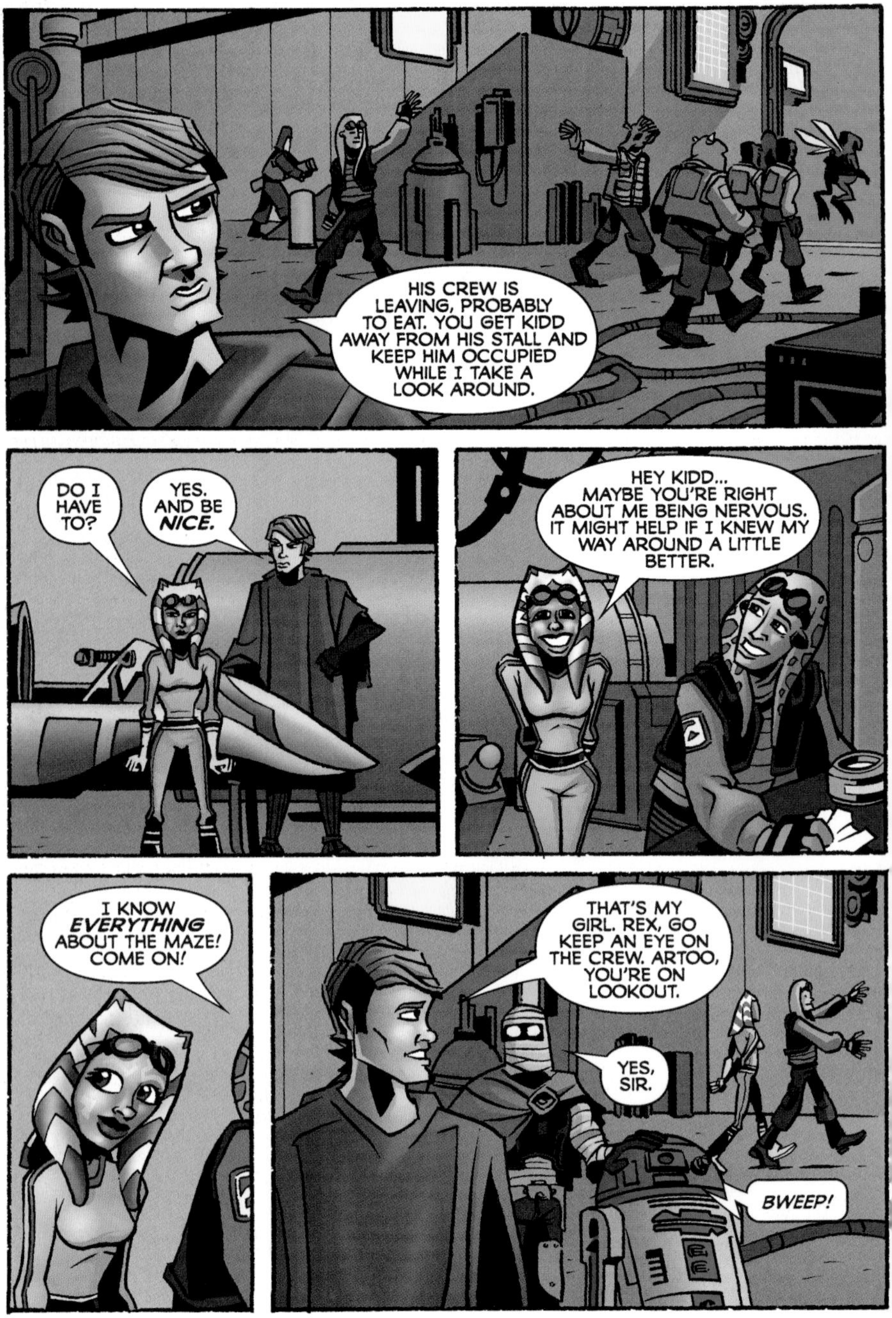
HIS CREW IS LEAVING, PROBABLY TO EAT. YOU GET KIDD AWAY FROM HIS STALL AND KEEP HIM OCCUPIED WHILE I TAKE A LOOK AROUND.
DO I HAVE TO?
YES. AND BE *NICE.*
HEY KIDD... MAYBE YOU'RE RIGHT ABOUT ME BEING NERVOUS. IT MIGHT HELP IF I KNEW MY WAY AROUND A LITTLE BETTER.
I KNOW *EVERYTHING* ABOUT THE MAZE! COME ON!
THAT'S MY GIRL. REX, GO KEEP AN EYE ON THE CREW. ARTOO, YOU'RE ON LOOKOUT.
YES, SIR.
BWEEP!

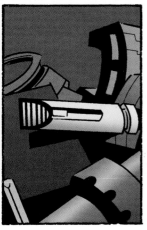

SEPARATIST COMLINK. GOTCHA.

BWEEP! BWEEP! BWEEP!

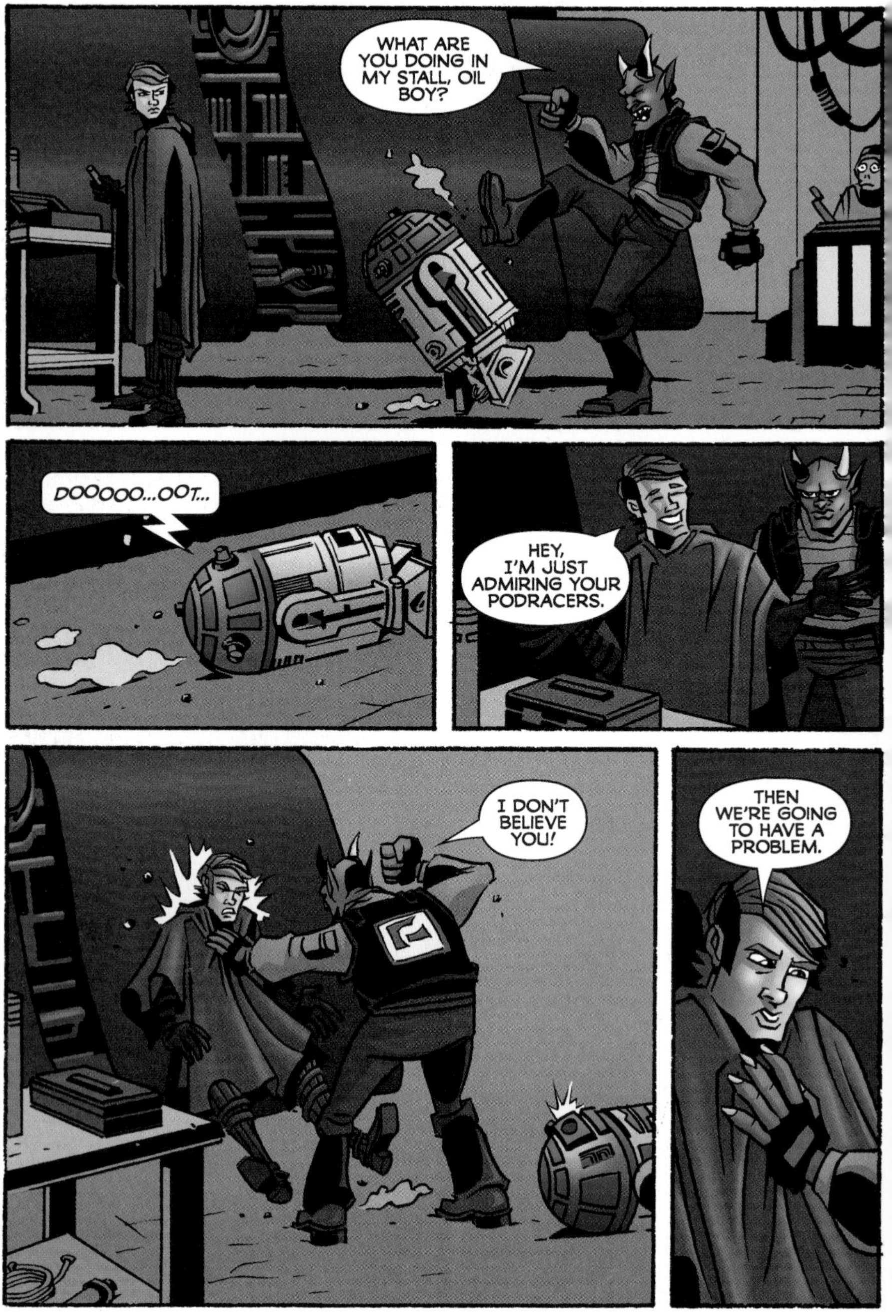
WHAT ARE YOU DOING IN MY STALL, OIL BOY?
DOOOOO...OOT...
HEY, I'M JUST ADMIRING YOUR PODRACERS.
I DON'T BELIEVE YOU!
THEN WE'RE GOING TO HAVE A PROBLEM.

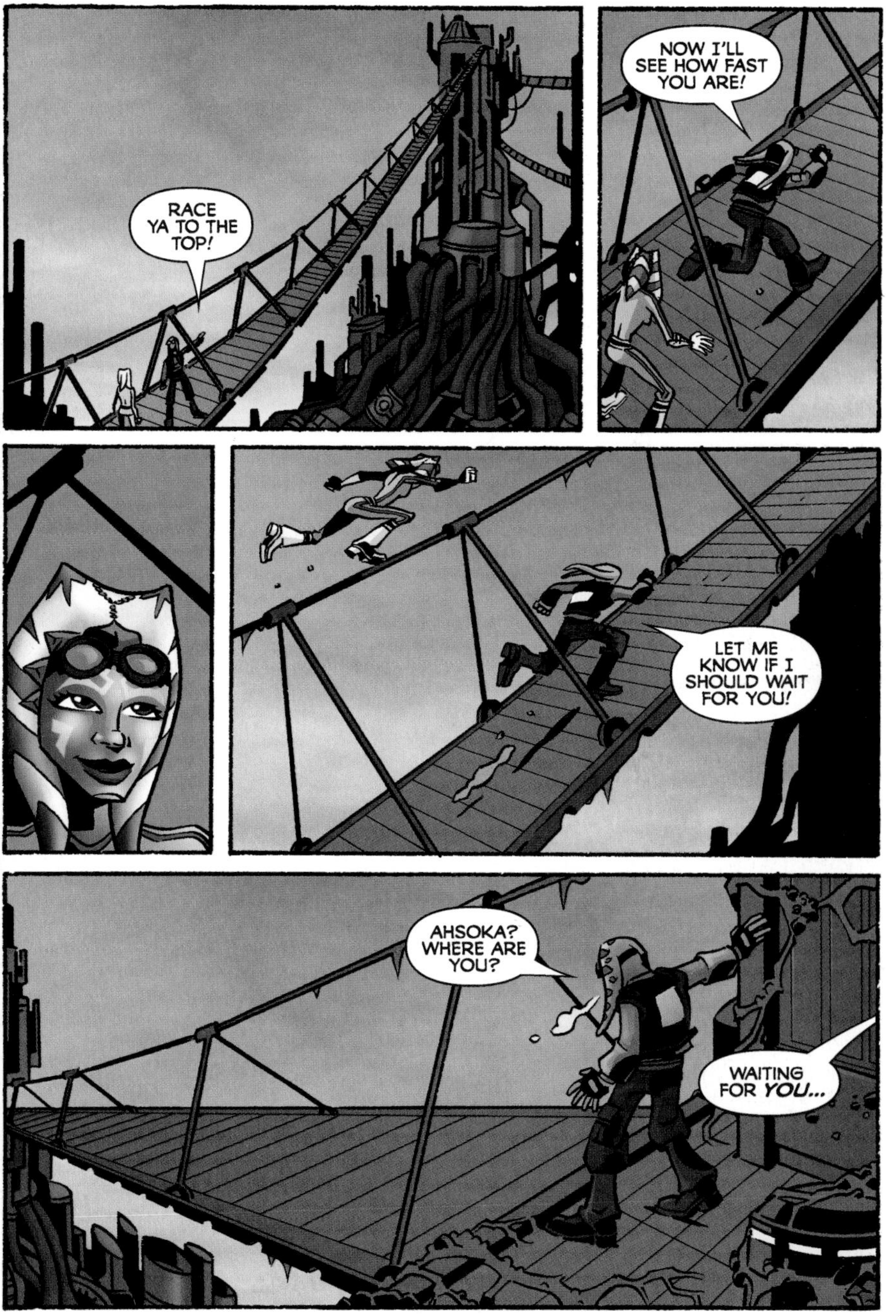
RACE YA TO THE TOP!
NOW I'LL SEE HOW FAST YOU ARE!
LET ME KNOW IF I SHOULD WAIT FOR YOU!
AHSOKA? WHERE ARE YOU?
WAITING FOR *YOU...*

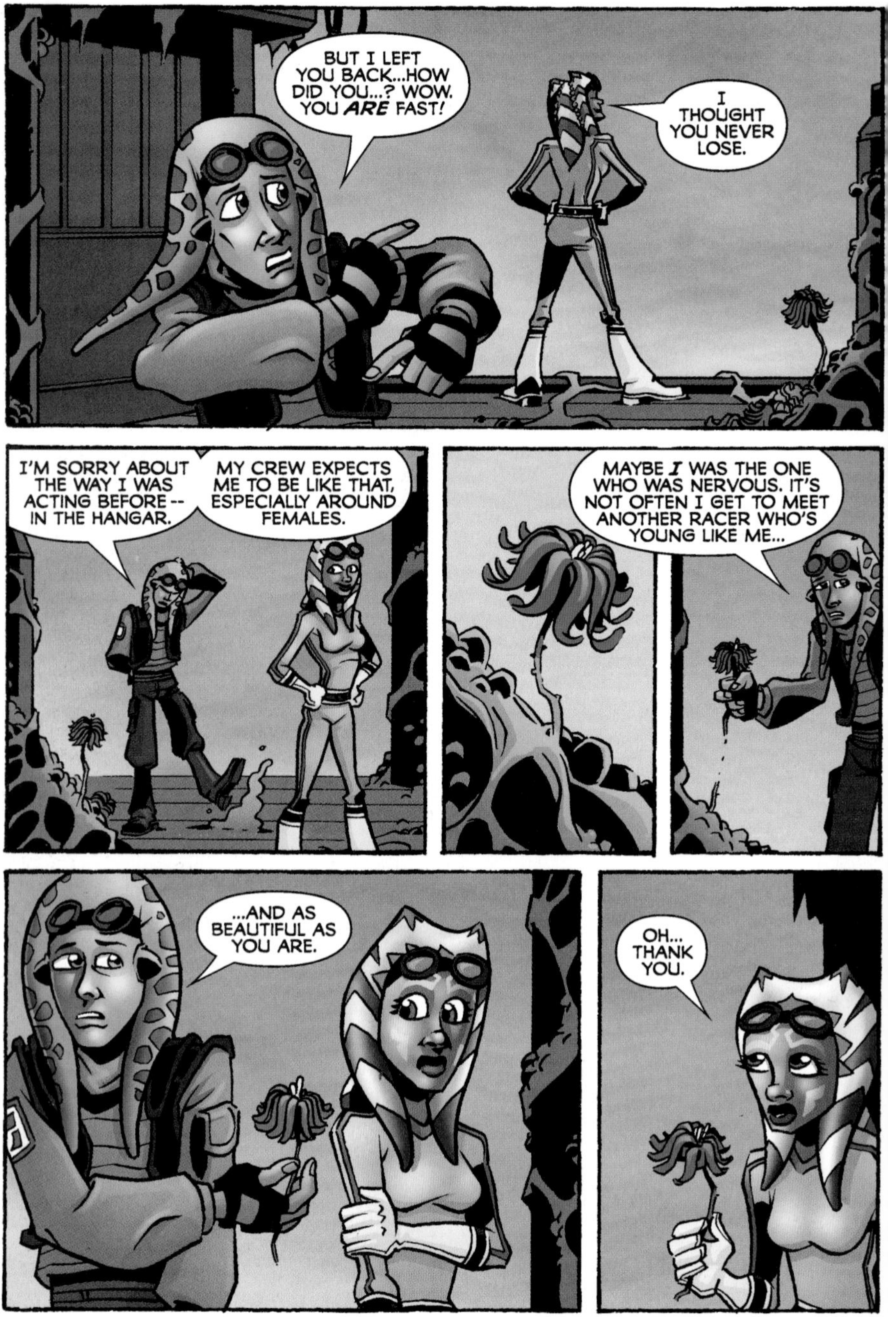
BUT I LEFT YOU BACK...HOW DID YOU...? WOW. YOU *ARE* FAST!
I THOUGHT YOU NEVER LOSE.
I'M SORRY ABOUT THE WAY I WAS ACTING BEFORE -- IN THE HANGAR.
MY CREW EXPECTS ME TO BE LIKE THAT, ESPECIALLY AROUND FEMALES.
MAYBE *I* WAS THE ONE WHO WAS NERVOUS. IT'S NOT OFTEN I GET TO MEET ANOTHER RACER WHO'S YOUNG LIKE ME...
...AND AS BEAUTIFUL AS YOU ARE.
OH... THANK YOU.

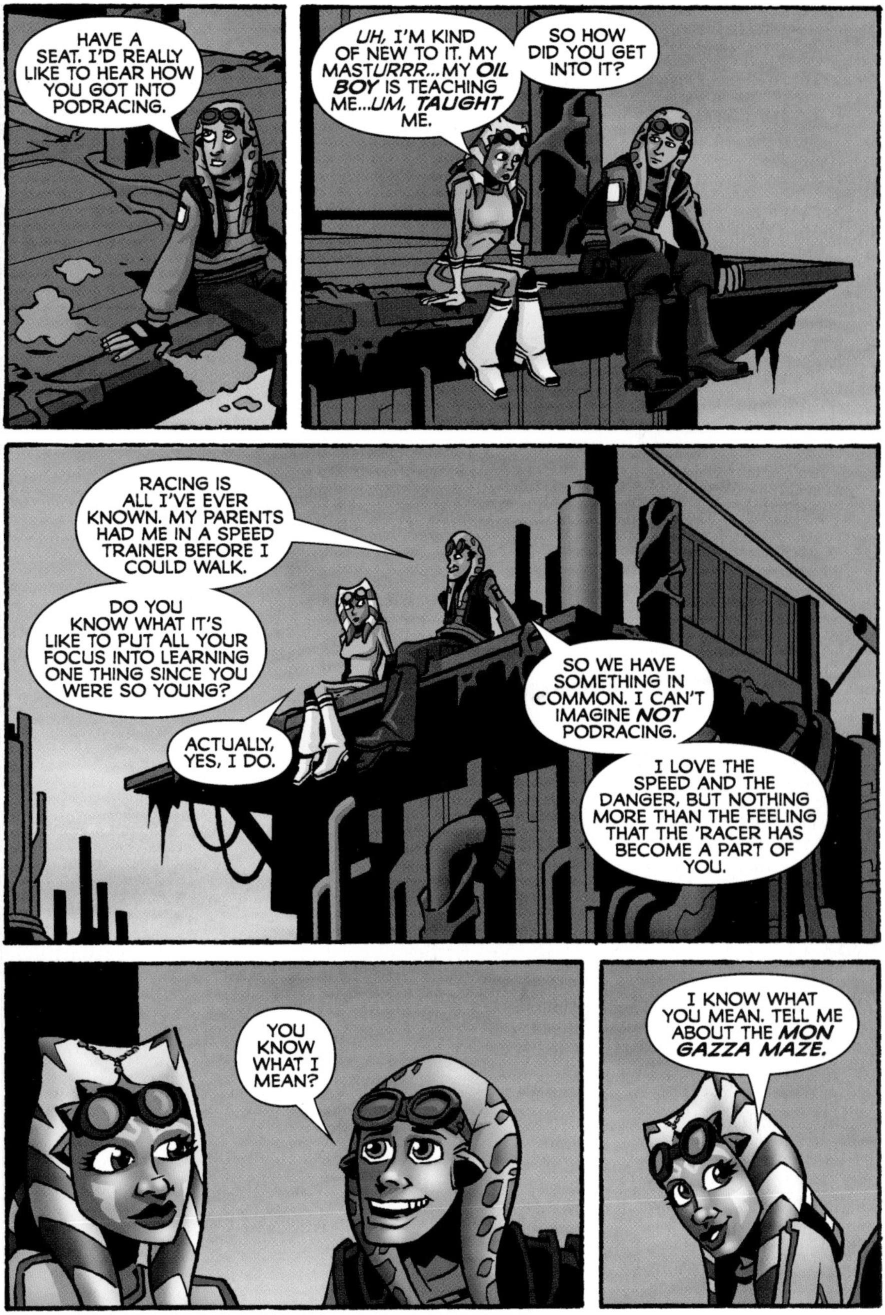
HAVE A SEAT. I'D REALLY LIKE TO HEAR HOW YOU GOT INTO PODRACING.
UH, I'M KIND OF NEW TO IT. MY MASTURRR...MY OIL BOY IS TEACHING ME...UM, TAUGHT ME.
SO HOW DID YOU GET INTO IT?
RACING IS ALL I'VE EVER KNOWN. MY PARENTS HAD ME IN A SPEED TRAINER BEFORE I COULD WALK.
DO YOU KNOW WHAT IT'S LIKE TO PUT ALL YOUR FOCUS INTO LEARNING ONE THING SINCE YOU WERE SO YOUNG?
ACTUALLY, YES, I DO.
SO WE HAVE SOMETHING IN COMMON. I CAN'T IMAGINE NOT PODRACING.
I LOVE THE SPEED AND THE DANGER, BUT NOTHING MORE THAN THE FEELING THAT THE 'RACER HAS BECOME A PART OF YOU.
YOU KNOW WHAT I MEAN?
I KNOW WHAT YOU MEAN. TELL ME ABOUT THE MON GAZZA MAZE.

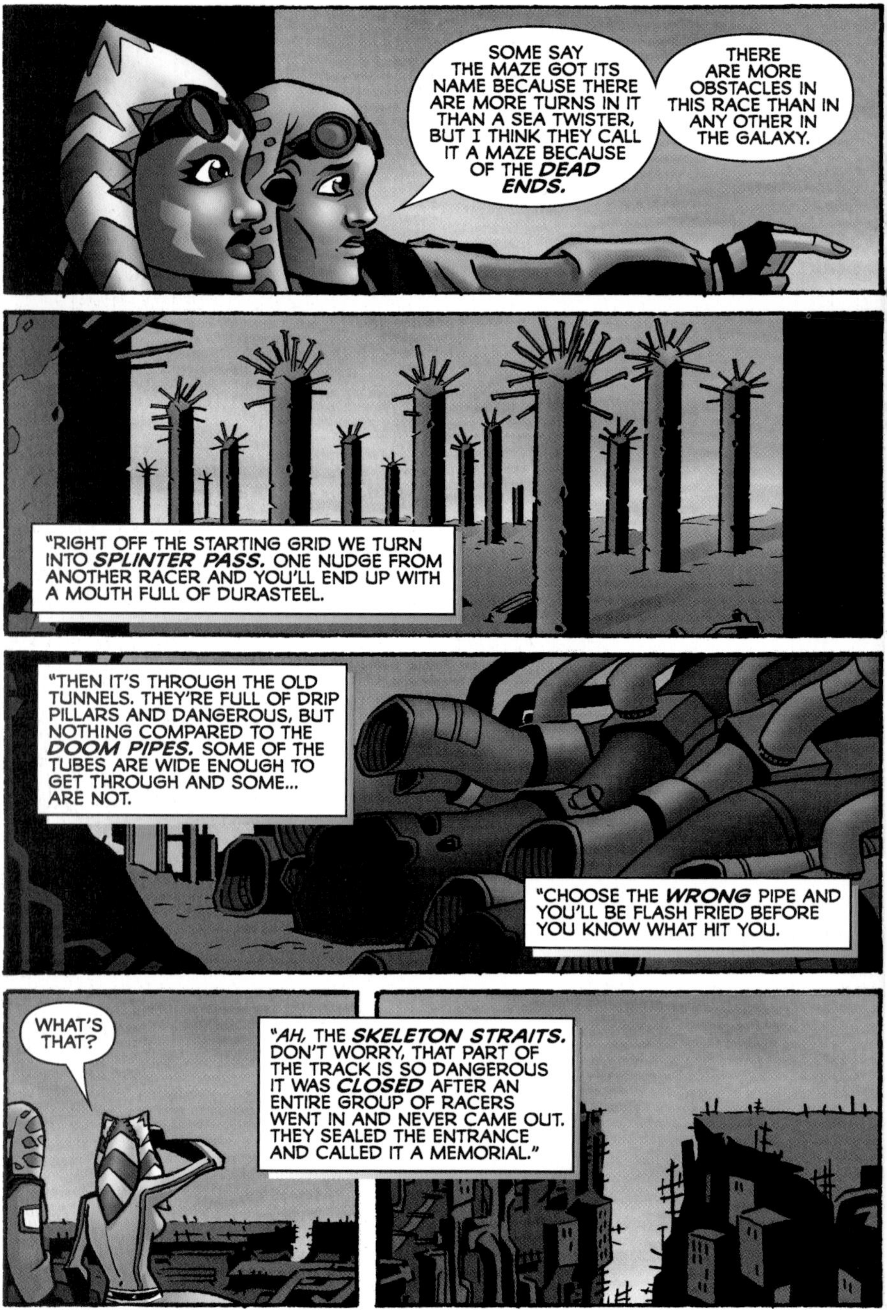
SOME SAY THE MAZE GOT ITS NAME BECAUSE THERE ARE MORE TURNS IN IT THAN A SEA TWISTER, BUT I THINK THEY CALL IT A MAZE BECAUSE OF THE *DEAD ENDS.*
THERE ARE MORE OBSTACLES IN THIS RACE THAN IN ANY OTHER IN THE GALAXY.
"RIGHT OFF THE STARTING GRID WE TURN INTO *SPLINTER PASS.* ONE NUDGE FROM ANOTHER RACER AND YOU'LL END UP WITH A MOUTH FULL OF DURASTEEL.
"THEN IT'S THROUGH THE OLD TUNNELS. THEY'RE FULL OF DRIP PILLARS AND DANGEROUS, BUT NOTHING COMPARED TO THE *DOOM PIPES.* SOME OF THE TUBES ARE WIDE ENOUGH TO GET THROUGH AND SOME... ARE NOT.
"CHOOSE THE *WRONG* PIPE AND YOU'LL BE FLASH FRIED BEFORE YOU KNOW WHAT HIT YOU.
WHAT'S THAT?
"*AH,* THE *SKELETON STRAITS.* DON'T WORRY, THAT PART OF THE TRACK IS SO DANGEROUS IT WAS *CLOSED* AFTER AN ENTIRE GROUP OF RACERS WENT IN AND NEVER CAME OUT. THEY SEALED THE ENTRANCE AND CALLED IT A MEMORIAL."

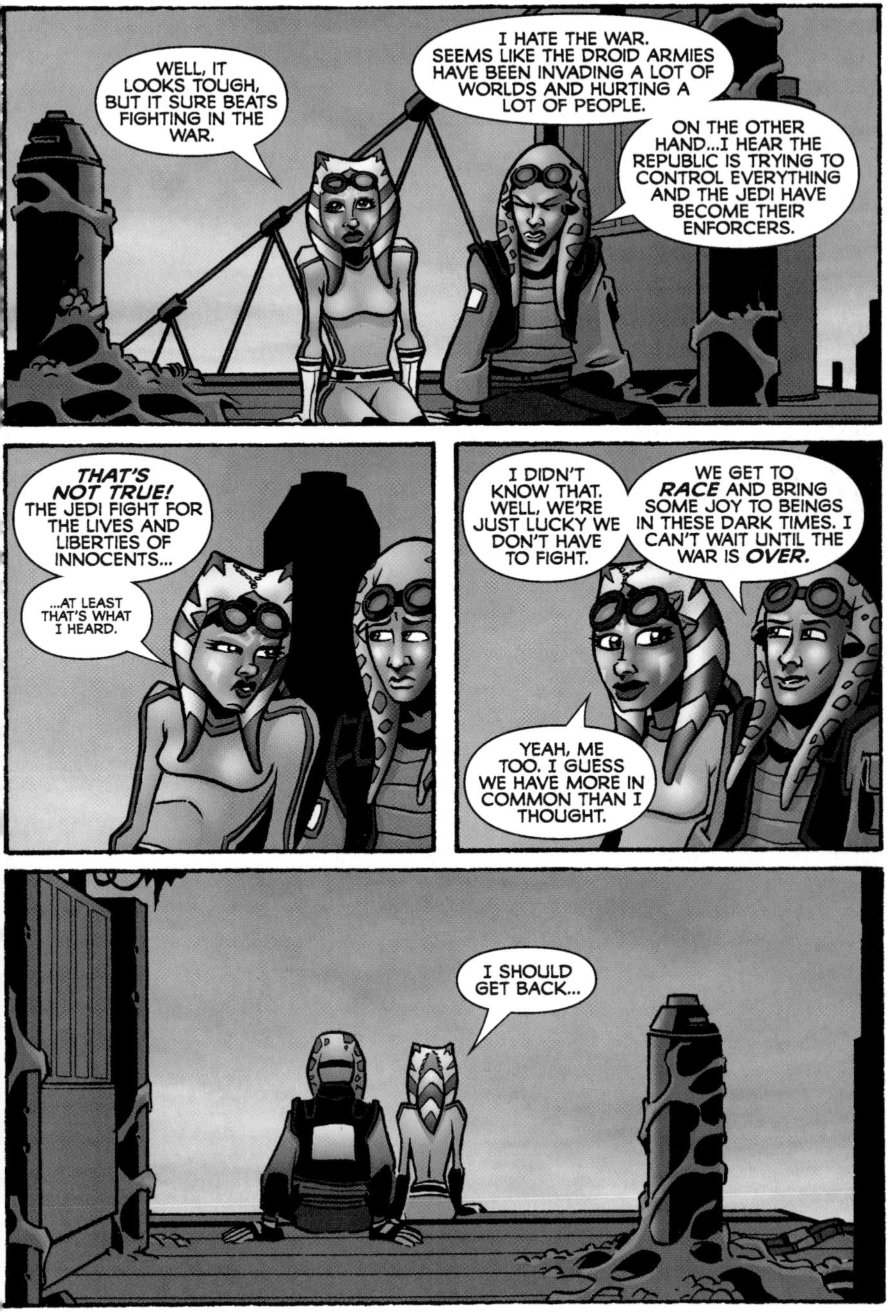
WELL, IT LOOKS TOUGH, BUT IT SURE BEATS FIGHTING IN THE WAR.
I HATE THE WAR. SEEMS LIKE THE DROID ARMIES HAVE BEEN INVADING A LOT OF WORLDS AND HURTING A LOT OF PEOPLE.
ON THE OTHER HAND...I HEAR THE REPUBLIC IS TRYING TO CONTROL EVERYTHING AND THE JEDI HAVE BECOME THEIR ENFORCERS.
THAT'S NOT TRUE! THE JEDI FIGHT FOR THE LIVES AND LIBERTIES OF INNOCENTS...
...AT LEAST THAT'S WHAT I HEARD.
I DIDN'T KNOW THAT. WELL, WE'RE JUST LUCKY WE DON'T HAVE TO FIGHT.
WE GET TO *RACE* AND BRING SOME JOY TO BEINGS IN THESE DARK TIMES. I CAN'T WAIT UNTIL THE WAR IS *OVER.*
YEAH, ME TOO. I GUESS WE HAVE MORE IN COMMON THAN I THOUGHT.
I SHOULD GET BACK...

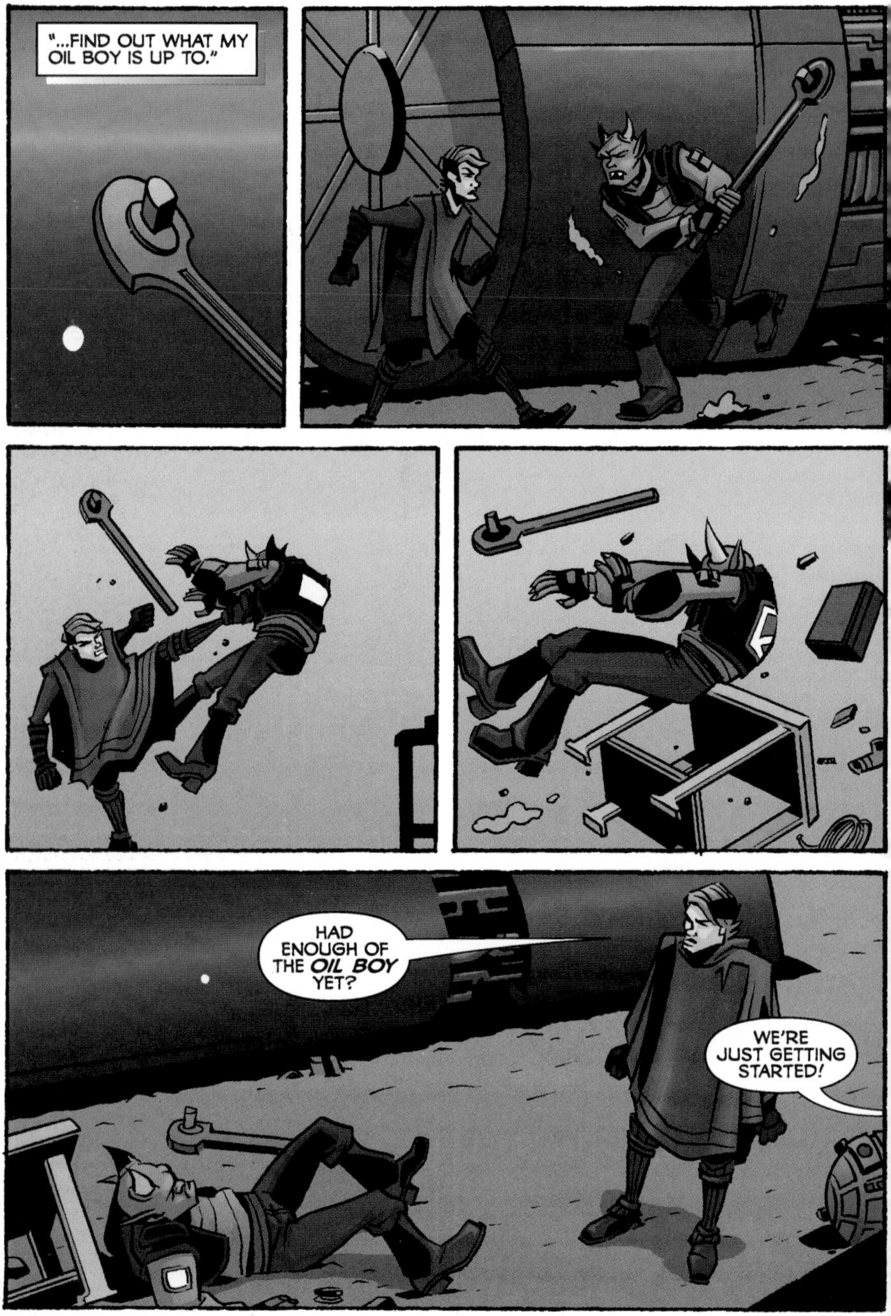
"...FIND OUT WHAT MY OIL BOY IS UP TO."
HAD ENOUGH OF THE *OIL BOY* YET?
WE'RE JUST GETTING STARTED!

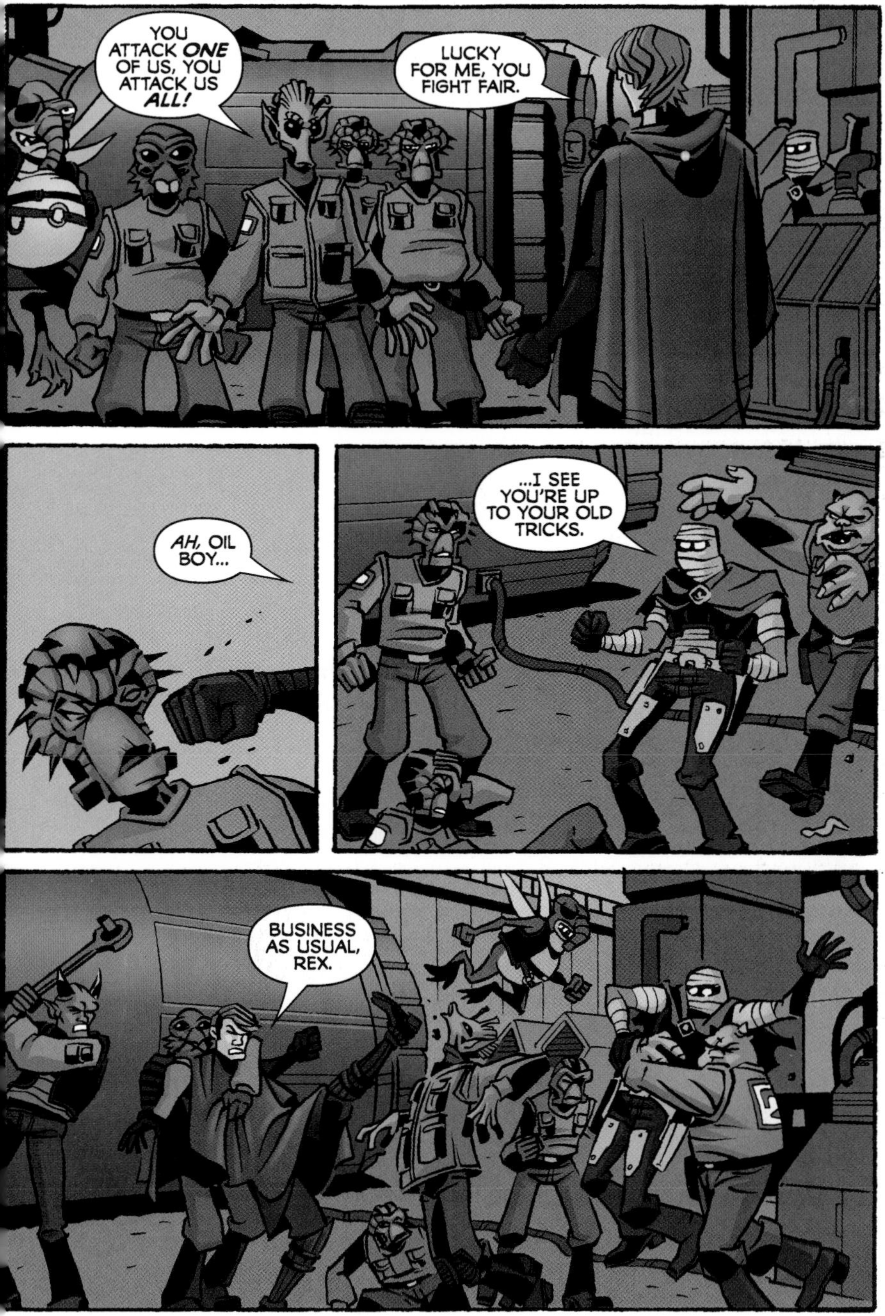
YOU ATTACK *ONE* OF US, YOU ATTACK US *ALL!*
LUCKY FOR ME, YOU FIGHT FAIR.
AH, OIL BOY...
...I SEE YOU'RE UP TO YOUR OLD TRICKS.
BUSINESS AS USUAL, REX.

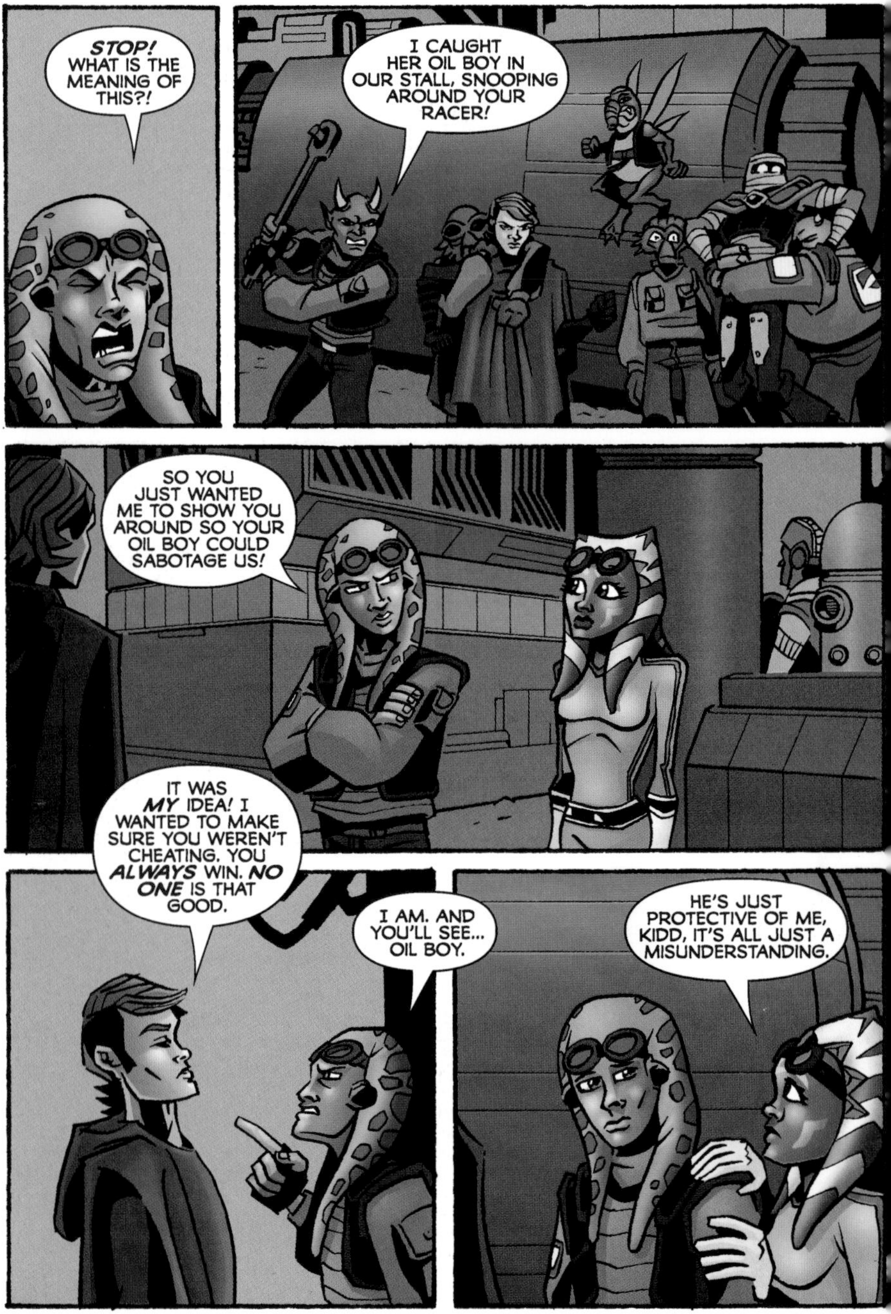
STOP! WHAT IS THE MEANING OF THIS?!
I CAUGHT HER OIL BOY IN OUR STALL, SNOOPING AROUND YOUR RACER!
SO YOU JUST WANTED ME TO SHOW YOU AROUND SO YOUR OIL BOY COULD SABOTAGE US!
IT WAS MY IDEA! I WANTED TO MAKE SURE YOU WEREN'T CHEATING. YOU ALWAYS WIN. NO ONE IS THAT GOOD.
I AM. AND YOU'LL SEE... OIL BOY.
HE'S JUST PROTECTIVE OF ME, KIDD, IT'S ALL JUST A MISUNDERSTANDING.

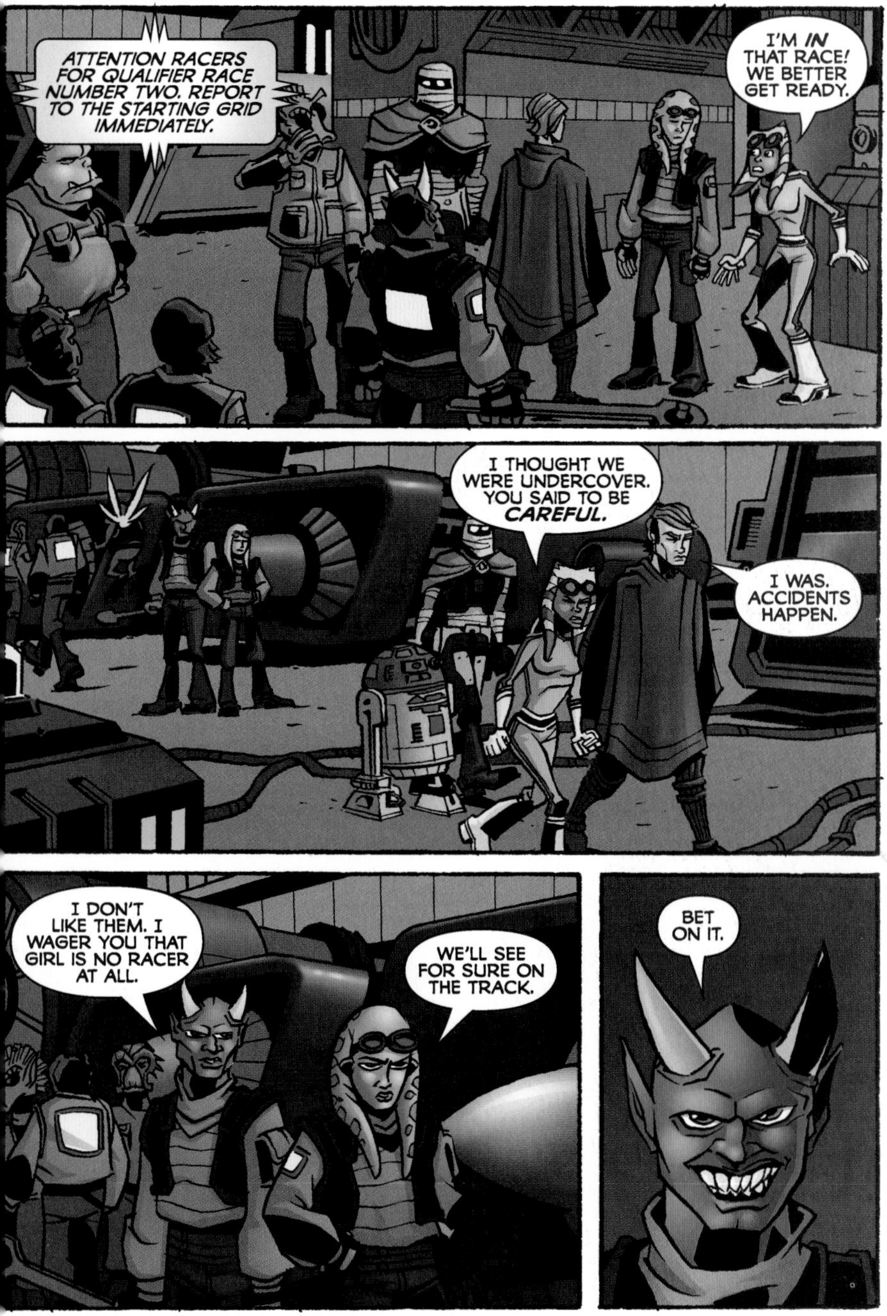
ATTENTION RACERS FOR QUALIFIER RACE NUMBER TWO. REPORT TO THE STARTING GRID IMMEDIATELY.
I'M *IN* THAT RACE! WE BETTER GET READY.
I THOUGHT WE WERE UNDERCOVER. YOU SAID TO BE ***CAREFUL.***
I WAS. ACCIDENTS HAPPEN.
I DON'T LIKE THEM. I WAGER YOU THAT GIRL IS NO RACER AT ALL.
WE'LL SEE FOR SURE ON THE TRACK.
BET ON IT.

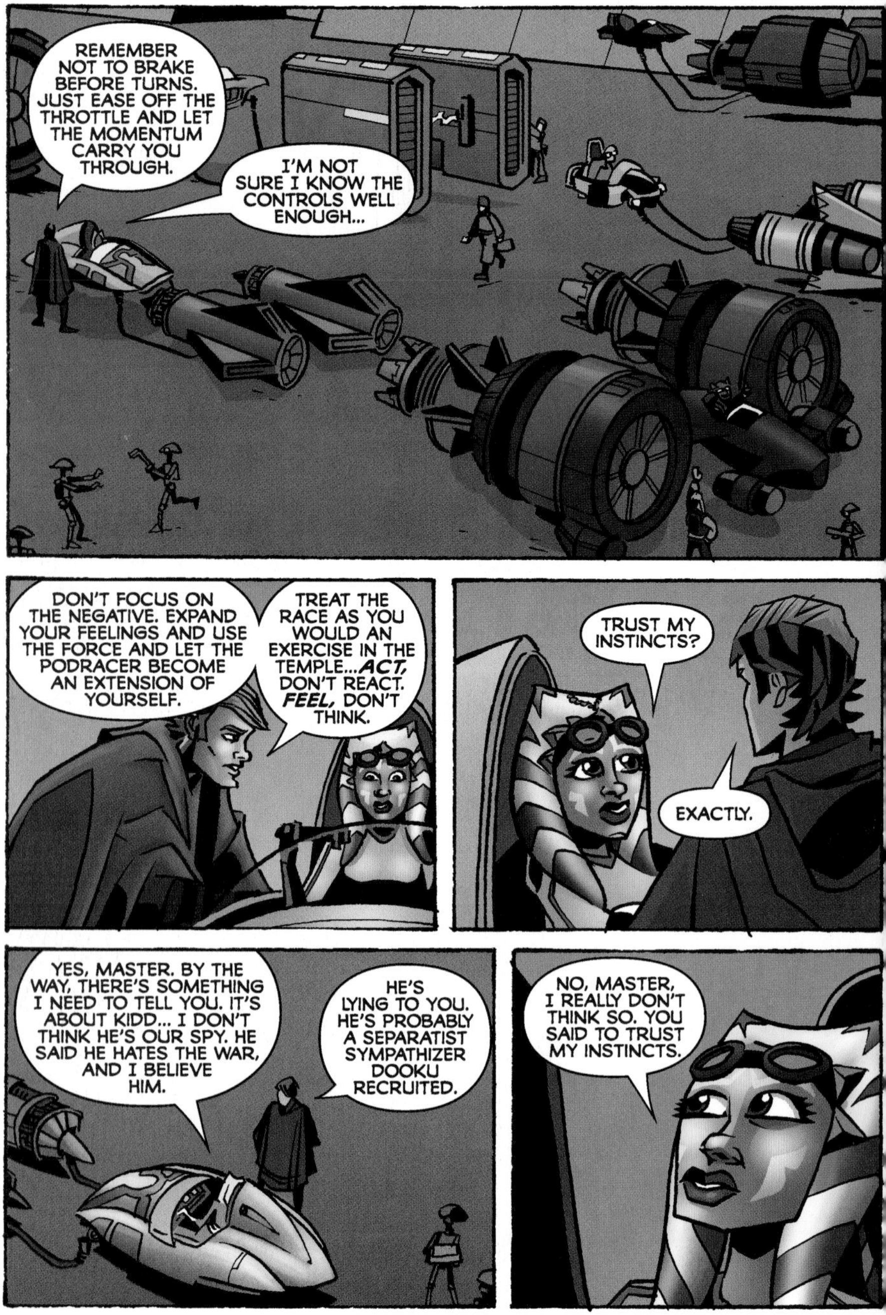
REMEMBER NOT TO BRAKE BEFORE TURNS. JUST EASE OFF THE THROTTLE AND LET THE MOMENTUM CARRY YOU THROUGH.
I'M NOT SURE I KNOW THE CONTROLS WELL ENOUGH...
DON'T FOCUS ON THE NEGATIVE. EXPAND YOUR FEELINGS AND USE THE FORCE AND LET THE PODRACER BECOME AN EXTENSION OF YOURSELF.
TREAT THE RACE AS YOU WOULD AN EXERCISE IN THE TEMPLE...*ACT,* DON'T REACT. *FEEL,* DON'T THINK.
TRUST MY INSTINCTS?
EXACTLY.
YES, MASTER. BY THE WAY, THERE'S SOMETHING I NEED TO TELL YOU. IT'S ABOUT KIDD... I DON'T THINK HE'S OUR SPY. HE SAID HE HATES THE WAR, AND I BELIEVE HIM.
HE'S LYING TO YOU. HE'S PROBABLY A SEPARATIST SYMPATHIZER DOOKU RECRUITED.
NO, MASTER, I REALLY DON'T THINK SO. YOU SAID TO TRUST MY INSTINCTS.

AHSOKA, DEVELOPING FEELINGS FOR HIM WILL CLOUD YOUR JUDGMENT. MAYBE I MADE A MISTAKE GIVING YOU THIS ASSIGNMENT.

WHY? BECAUSE I DISAGREE WITH YOU? YOU TELL ME TO TRUST MY INSTINCTS AND WHEN I DO, YOU REACT LIKE THIS. NOT EVERYTHING IS BLACK AND WHITE! YOU ALWAYS JUMP TO CONCLUSIONS.

DID YOU FIND THE DATA FILE IN THEIR STALL?

NO, BUT I FOUND A SEPARATIST COMLINK.

WHAT DOES THAT PROVE? YOU KNOW HOW MANY OTHER FACTIONS ALSO USE THAT STYLE OF COMLINK?

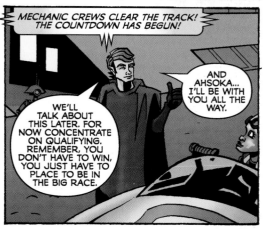

MECHANIC CREWS CLEAR THE TRACK! THE COUNTDOWN HAS BEGUN!

AND AHSOKA... I'LL BE WITH YOU ALL THE WAY.

WE'LL TALK ABOUT THIS LATER. FOR NOW CONCENTRATE ON QUALIFYING. REMEMBER, YOU DON'T HAVE TO WIN, YOU JUST HAVE TO PLACE TO BE IN THE BIG RACE.

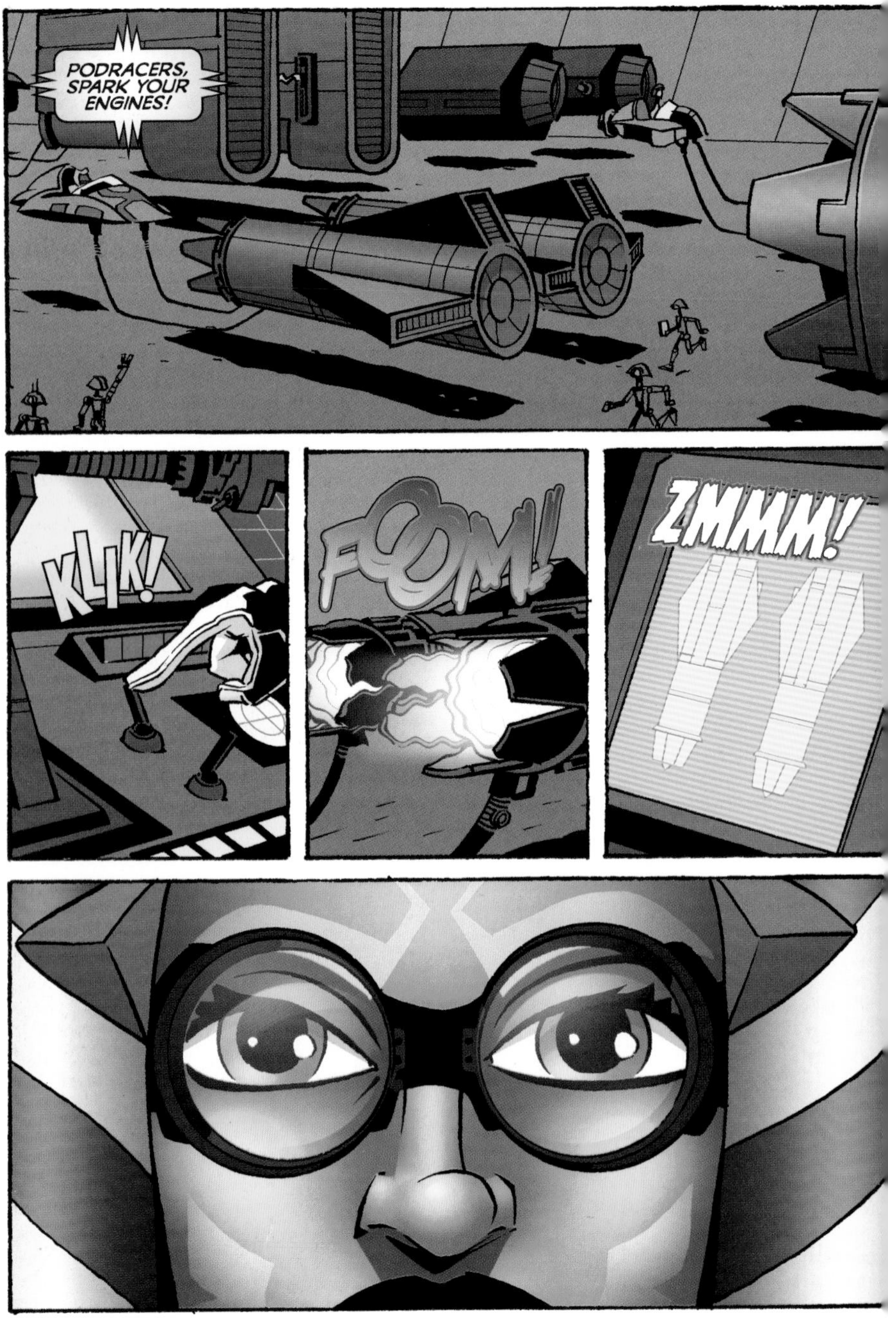
PODRACERS, SPARK YOUR ENGINES!
KLIK!
FOOM!
ZMMM!

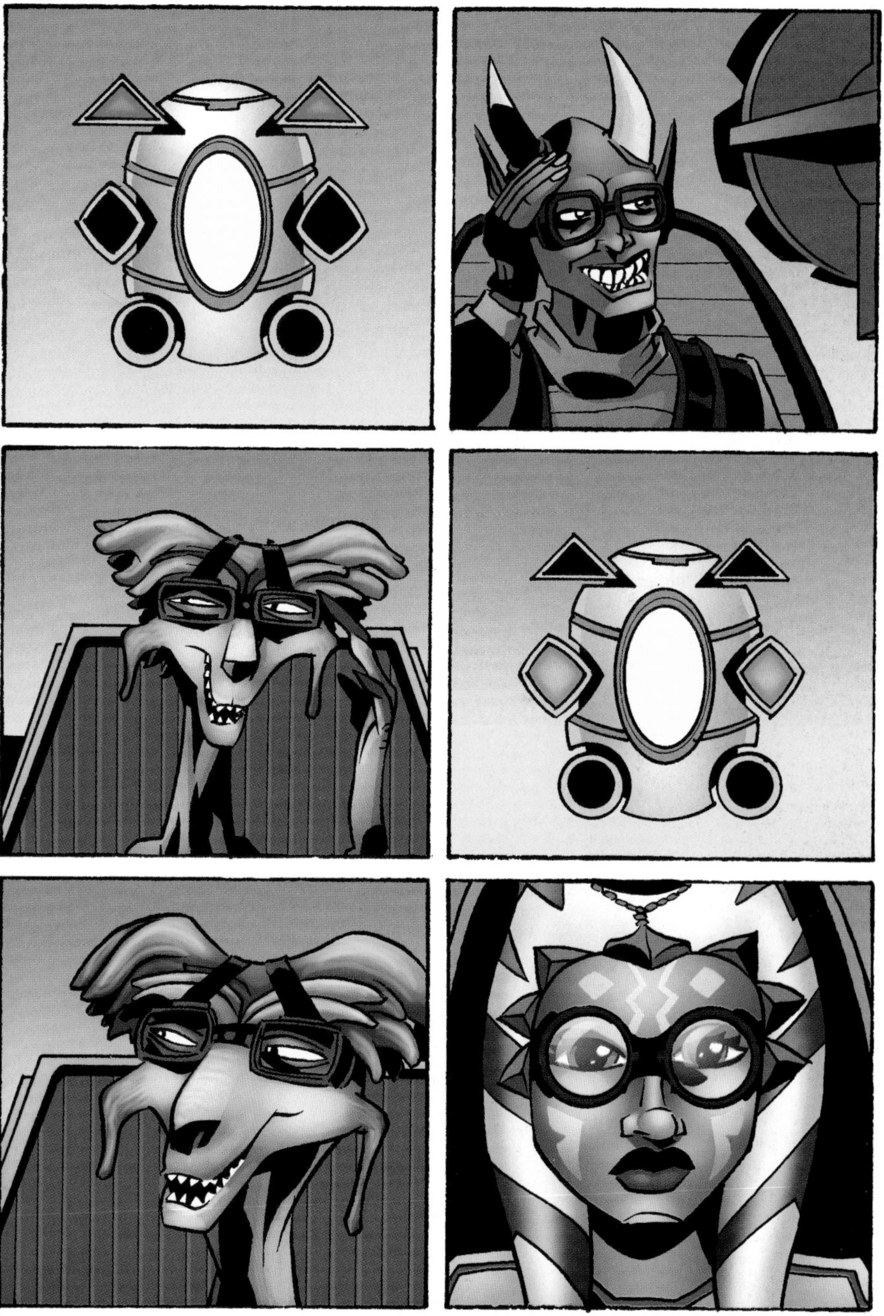

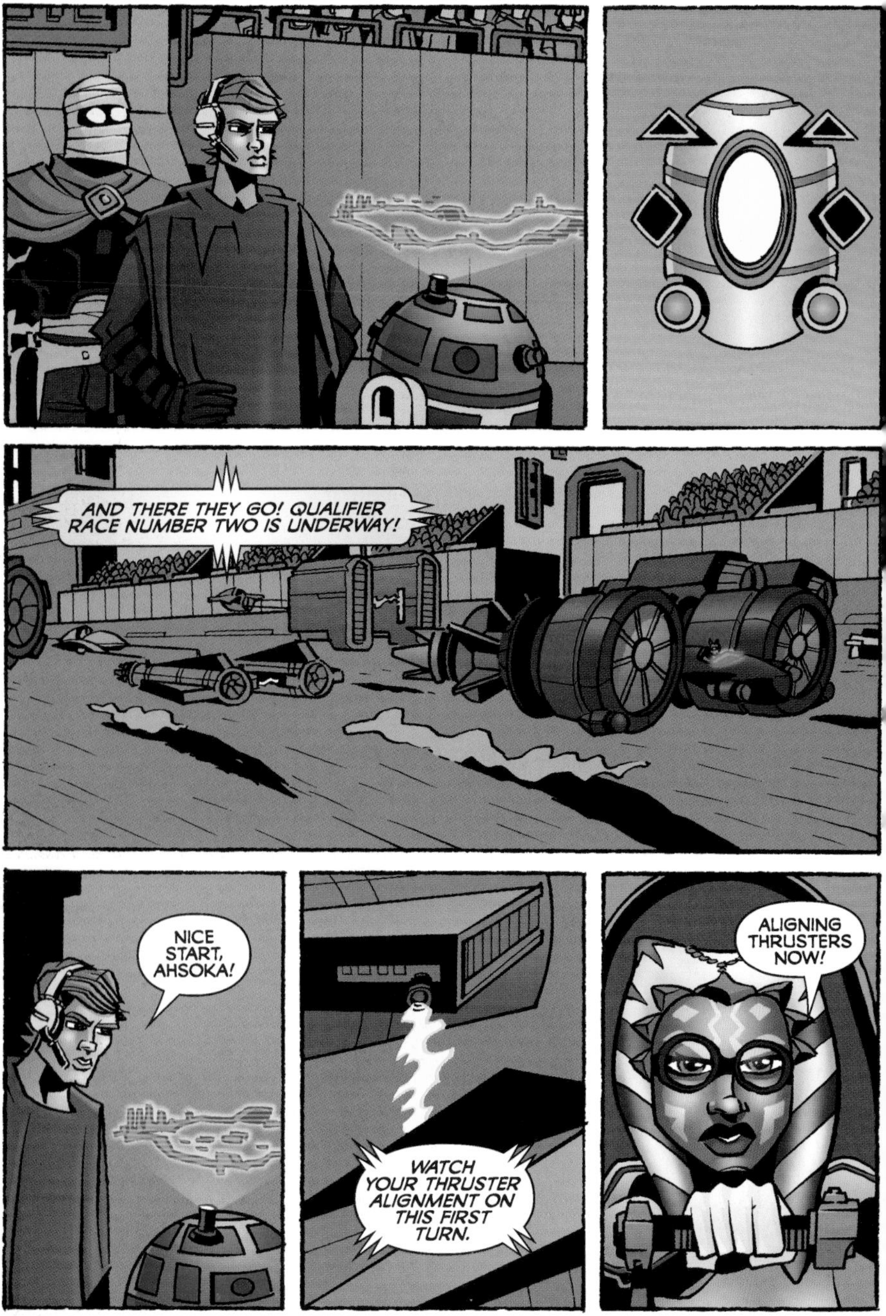
AND THERE THEY GO! QUALIFIER RACE NUMBER TWO IS UNDERWAY!
NICE START, AHSOKA!
WATCH YOUR THRUSTER ALIGNMENT ON THIS FIRST TURN.
ALIGNING THRUSTERS NOW!

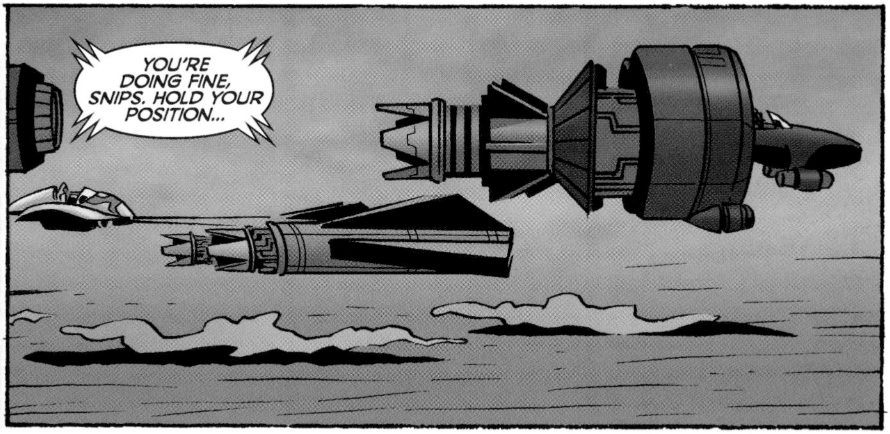
YOU'RE DOING FINE, SNIPS. HOLD YOUR POSITION...

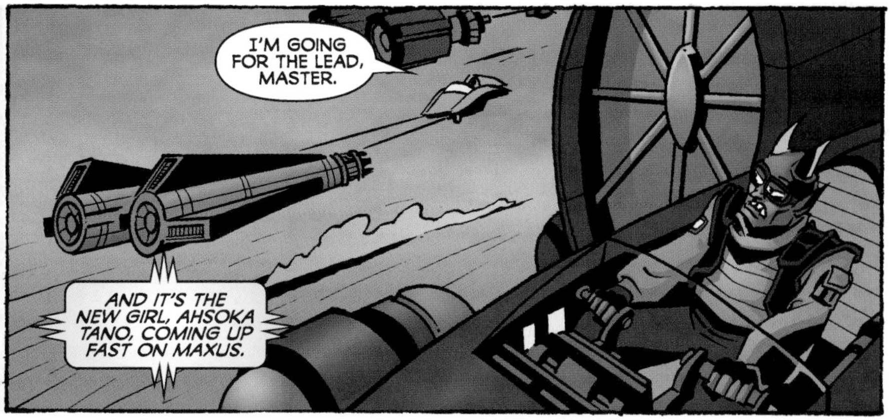
I'M GOING FOR THE LEAD, MASTER.
AND IT'S THE NEW GIRL, AHSOKA TANO, COMING UP FAST ON MAXUS.

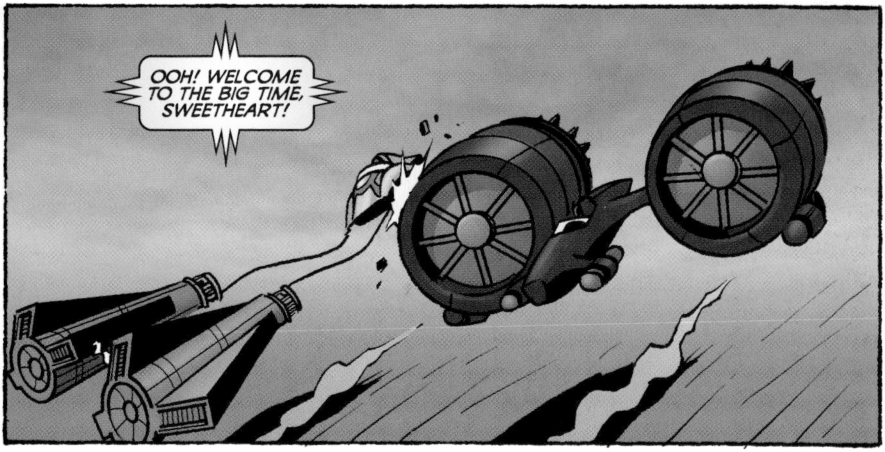
OOH! WELCOME TO THE BIG TIME, SWEETHEART!

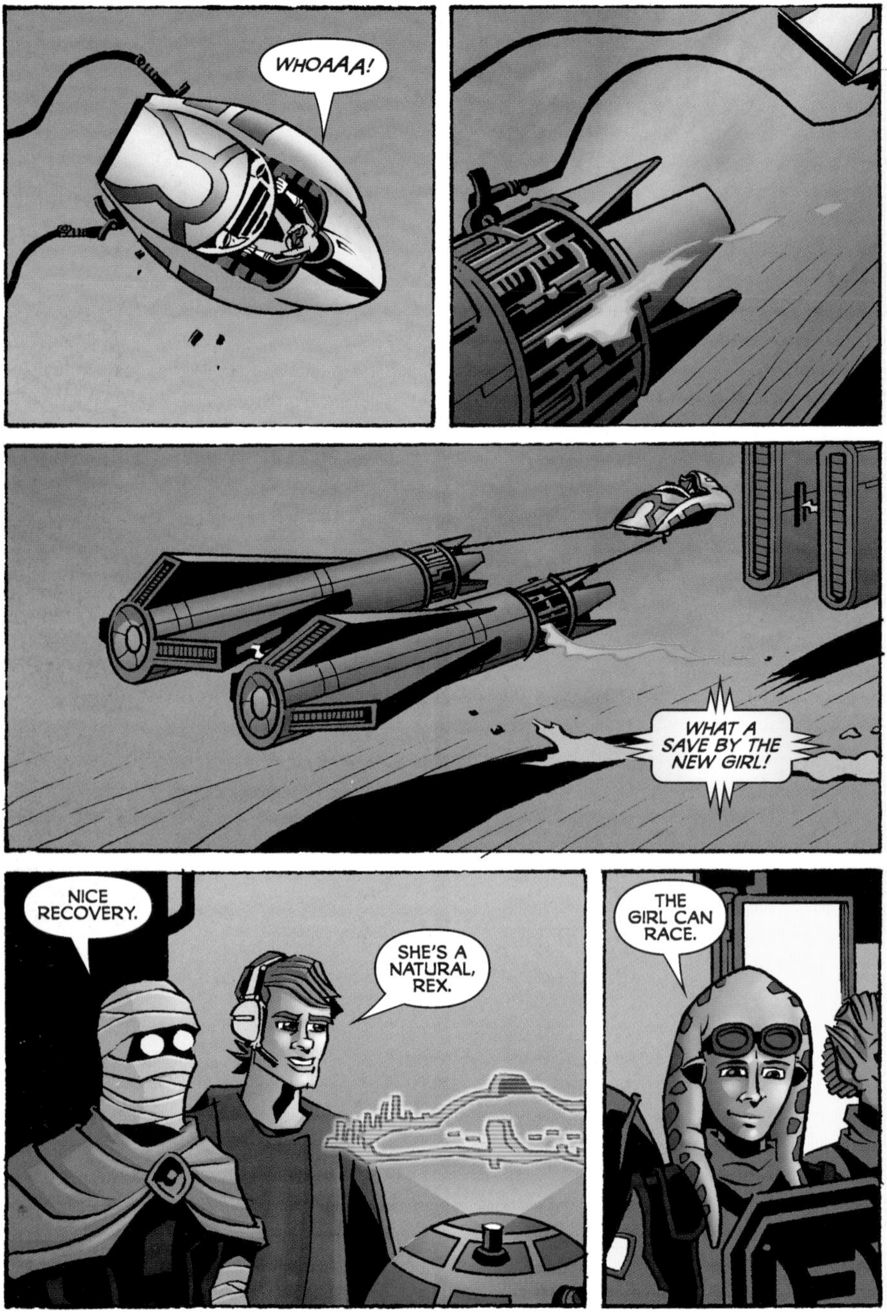
WHOAAA!
WHAT A SAVE BY THE NEW GIRL!
NICE RECOVERY.
SHE'S A NATURAL, REX.
THE GIRL CAN RACE.

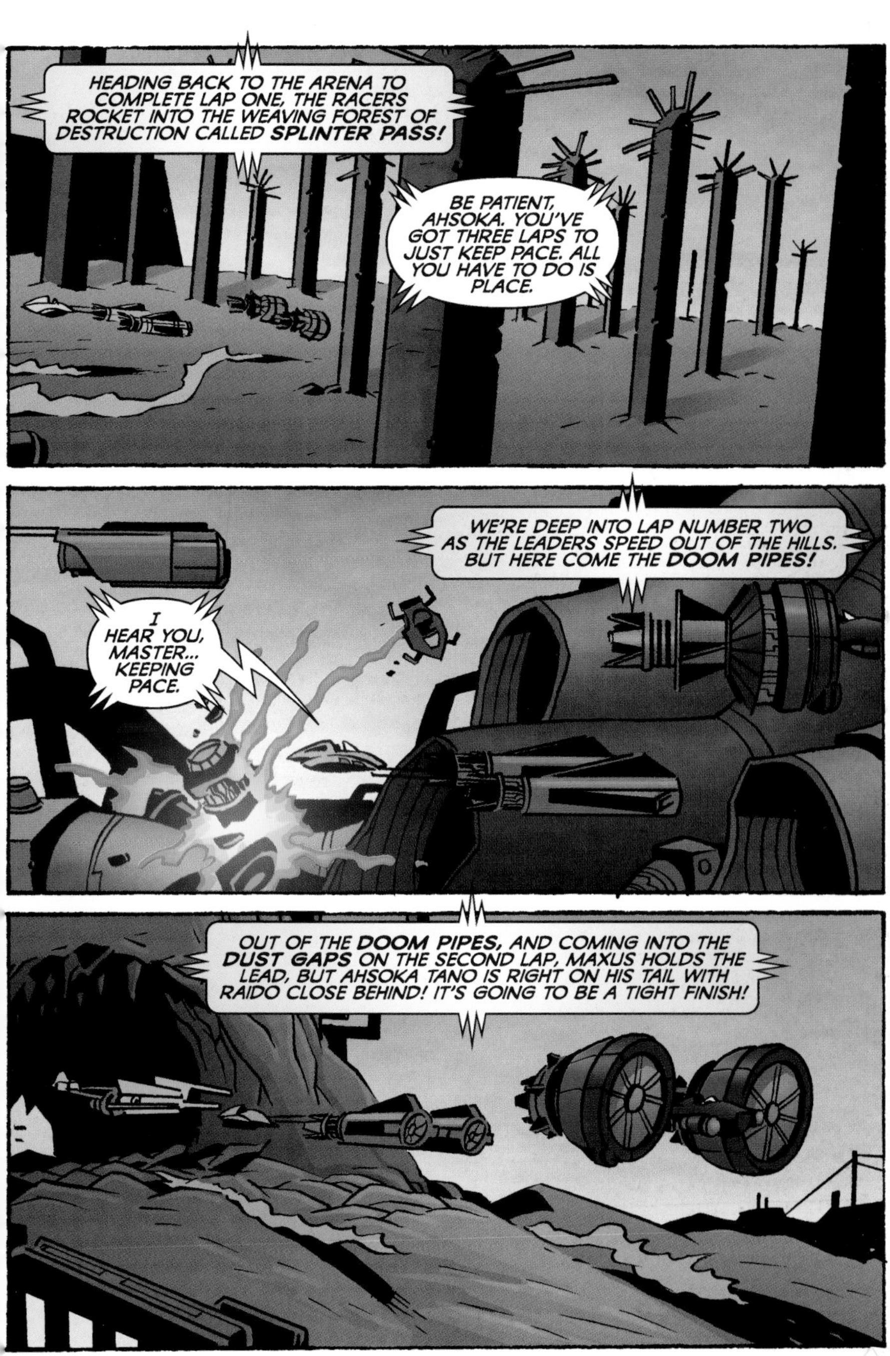

HEADING BACK TO THE ARENA TO COMPLETE LAP ONE, THE RACERS ROCKET INTO THE WEAVING FOREST OF DESTRUCTION CALLED **SPLINTER PASS!**
BE PATIENT, AHSOKA. YOU'VE GOT THREE LAPS TO JUST KEEP PACE. ALL YOU HAVE TO DO IS PLACE.
WE'RE DEEP INTO LAP NUMBER TWO AS THE LEADERS SPEED OUT OF THE HILLS. BUT HERE COME THE **DOOM PIPES!**
I HEAR YOU, MASTER... KEEPING PACE.
OUT OF THE **DOOM PIPES,** AND COMING INTO THE **DUST GAPS** ON THE SECOND LAP, MAXUS HOLDS THE LEAD, BUT AHSOKA TANO IS RIGHT ON HIS TAIL WITH RAIDO CLOSE BEHIND! IT'S GOING TO BE A TIGHT FINISH!

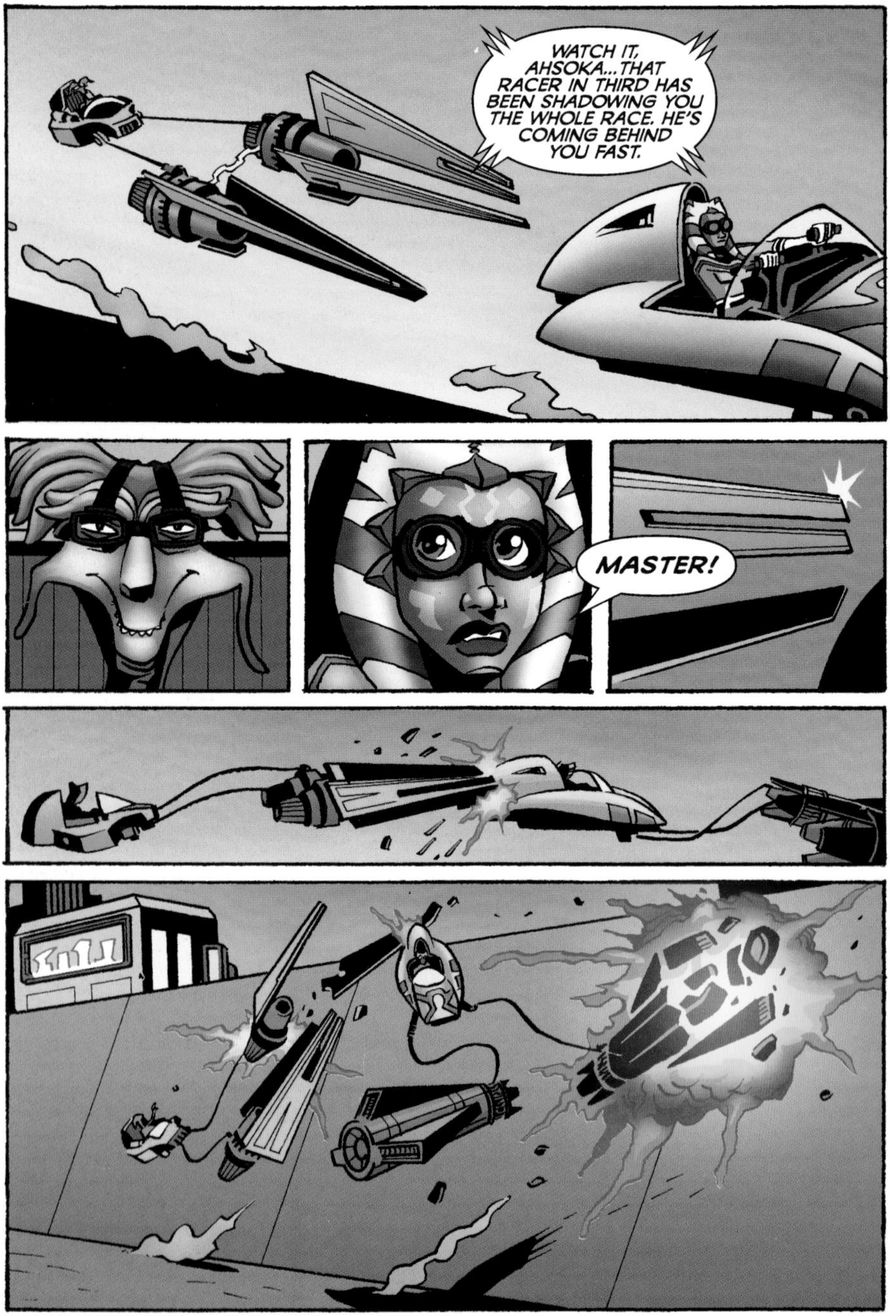
WATCH IT, AHSOKA...THAT RACER IN THIRD HAS BEEN SHADOWING YOU THE WHOLE RACE. HE'S COMING BEHIND YOU FAST.
MASTER!

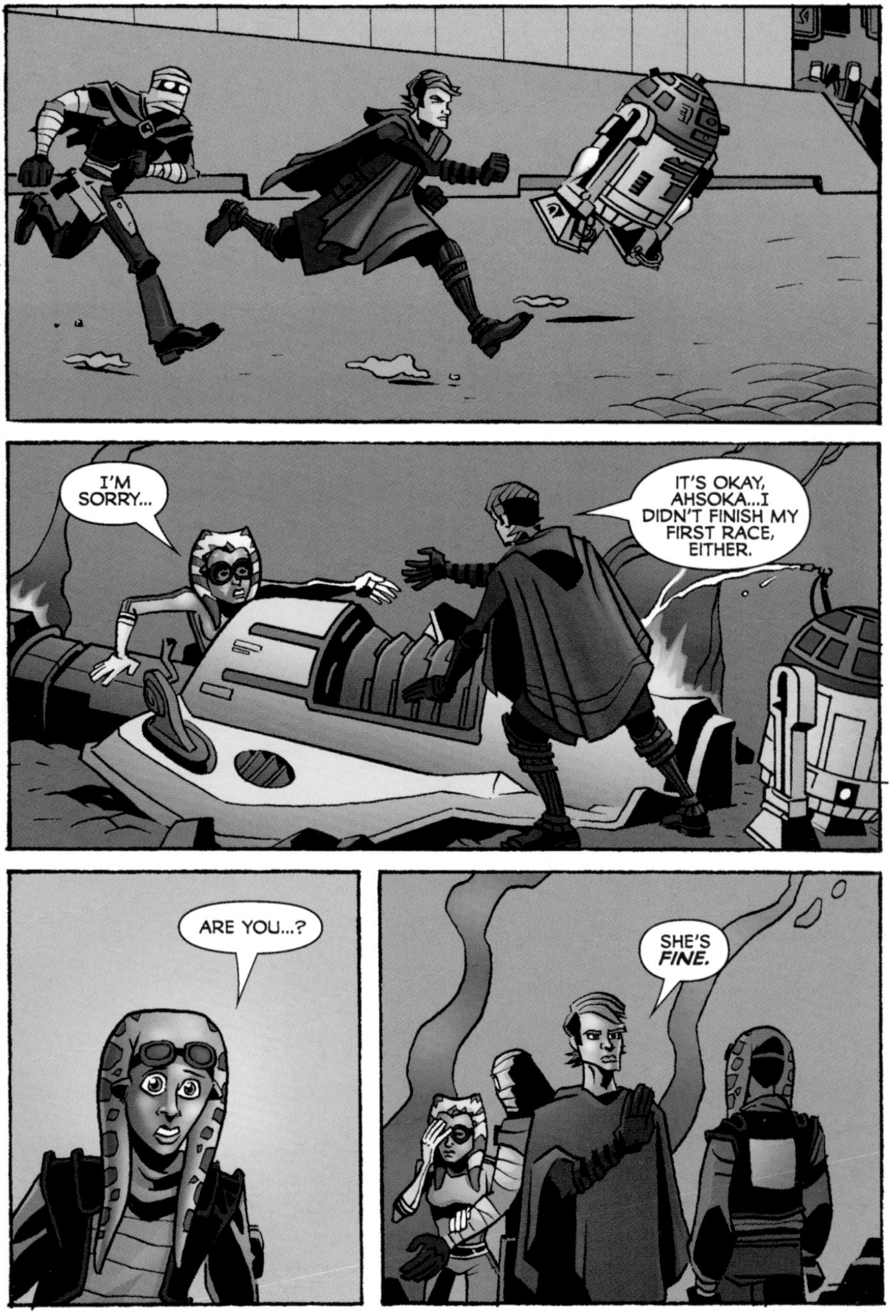
I'M SORRY...
IT'S OKAY, AHSOKA...I DIDN'T FINISH MY FIRST RACE, EITHER.
ARE YOU...?
SHE'S *FINE.*

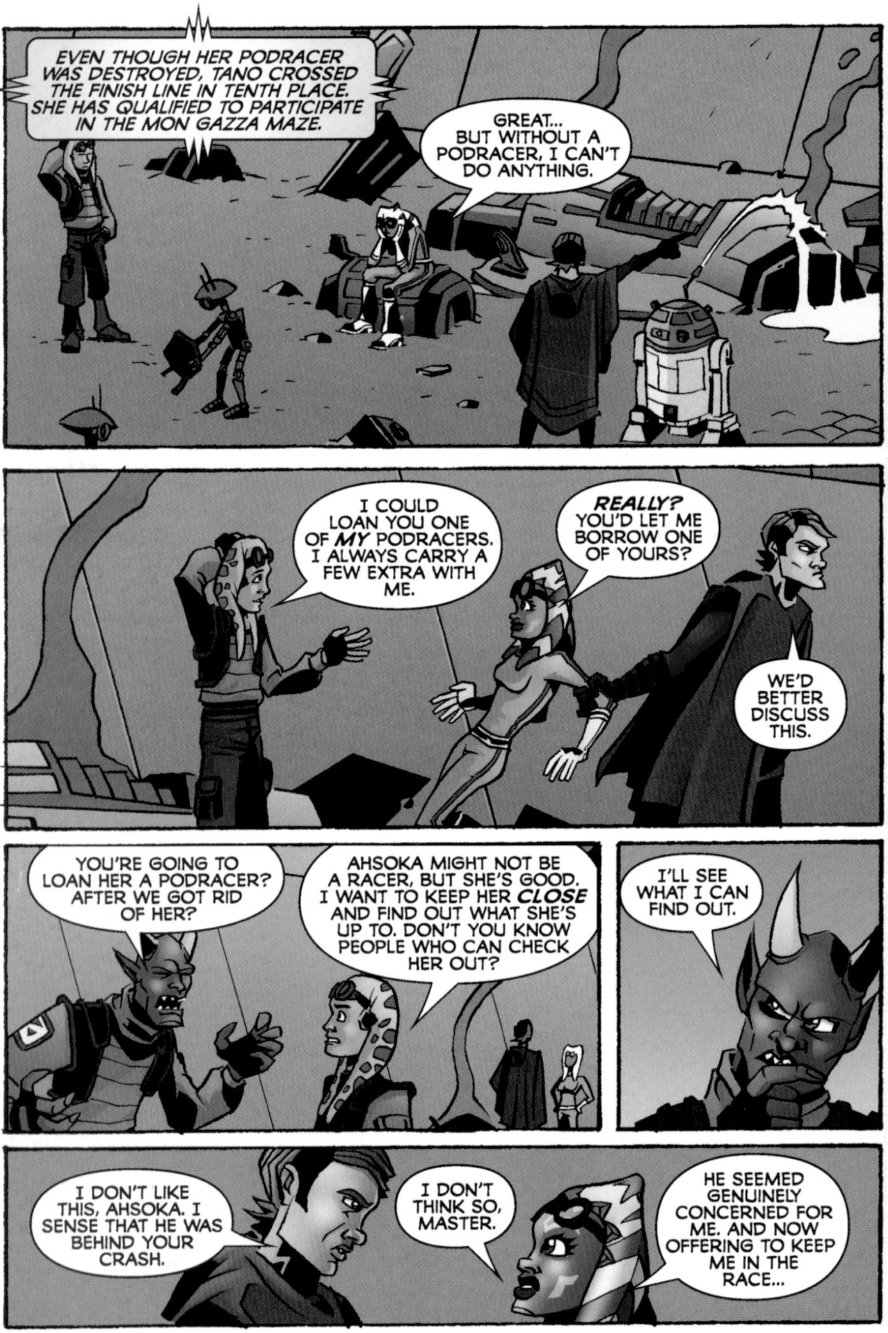
EVEN THOUGH HER PODRACER WAS DESTROYED, TANO CROSSED THE FINISH LINE IN TENTH PLACE. SHE HAS QUALIFIED TO PARTICIPATE IN THE MON GAZZA MAZE.
GREAT... BUT WITHOUT A PODRACER, I CAN'T DO ANYTHING.
I COULD LOAN YOU ONE OF *MY* PODRACERS. I ALWAYS CARRY A FEW EXTRA WITH ME.
REALLY? YOU'D LET ME BORROW ONE OF YOURS?
WE'D BETTER DISCUSS THIS.
YOU'RE GOING TO LOAN HER A PODRACER? AFTER WE GOT RID OF HER?
AHSOKA MIGHT NOT BE A RACER, BUT SHE'S GOOD. I WANT TO KEEP HER *CLOSE* AND FIND OUT WHAT SHE'S UP TO. DON'T YOU KNOW PEOPLE WHO CAN CHECK HER OUT?
I'LL SEE WHAT I CAN FIND OUT.
I DON'T LIKE THIS, AHSOKA. I SENSE THAT HE WAS BEHIND YOUR CRASH.
I DON'T THINK SO, MASTER.
HE SEEMED GENUINELY CONCERNED FOR ME. AND NOW OFFERING TO KEEP ME IN THE RACE...

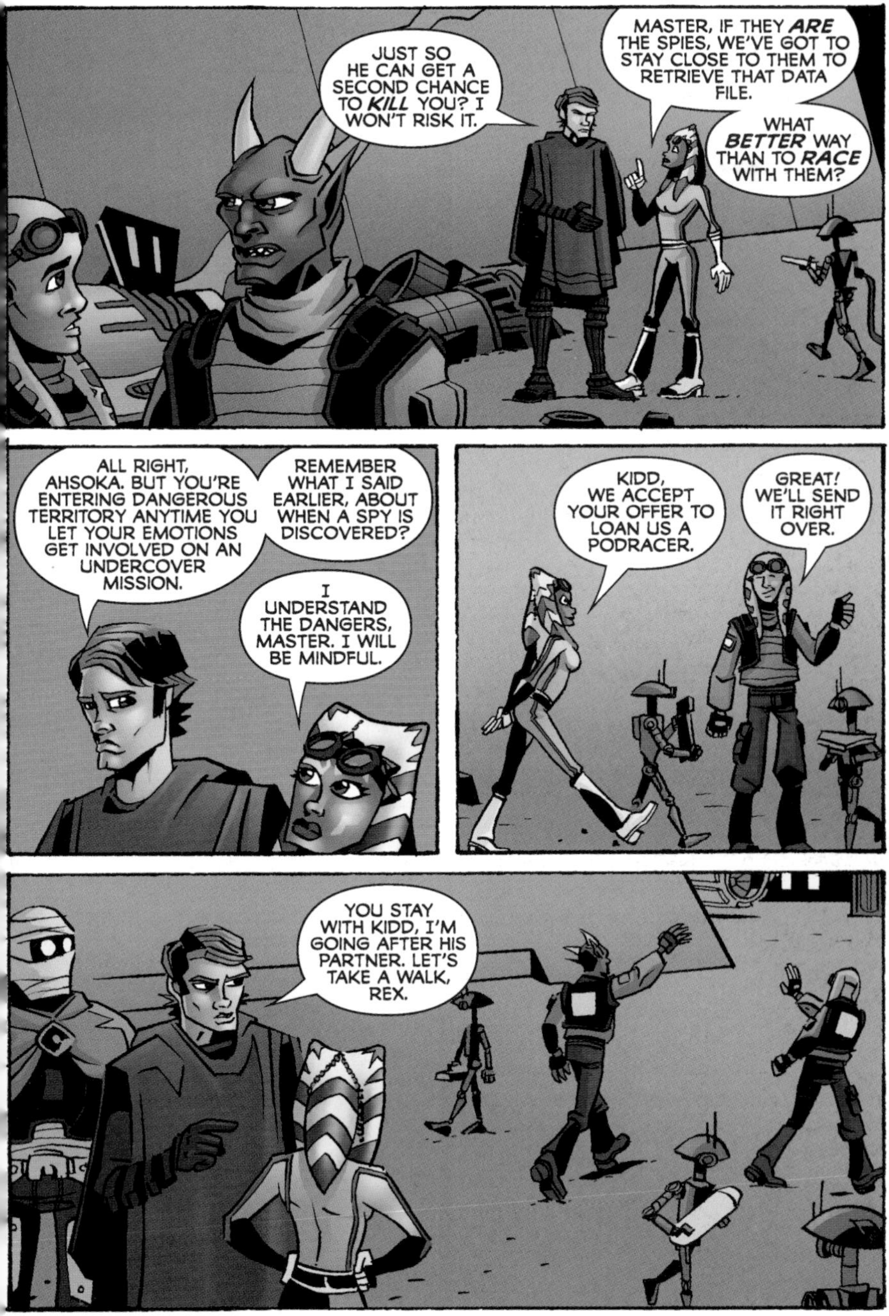
JUST SO HE CAN GET A SECOND CHANCE TO *KILL* YOU? I WON'T RISK IT.
MASTER, IF THEY *ARE* THE SPIES, WE'VE GOT TO STAY CLOSE TO THEM TO RETRIEVE THAT DATA FILE.
WHAT *BETTER* WAY THAN TO *RACE* WITH THEM?
ALL RIGHT, AHSOKA. BUT YOU'RE ENTERING DANGEROUS TERRITORY ANYTIME YOU LET YOUR EMOTIONS GET INVOLVED ON AN UNDERCOVER MISSION.
REMEMBER WHAT I SAID EARLIER, ABOUT WHEN A SPY IS DISCOVERED?
I UNDERSTAND THE DANGERS, MASTER. I WILL BE MINDFUL.
KIDD, WE ACCEPT YOUR OFFER TO LOAN US A PODRACER.
GREAT! WE'LL SEND IT RIGHT OVER.
YOU STAY WITH KIDD, I'M GOING AFTER HIS PARTNER. LET'S TAKE A WALK, REX.

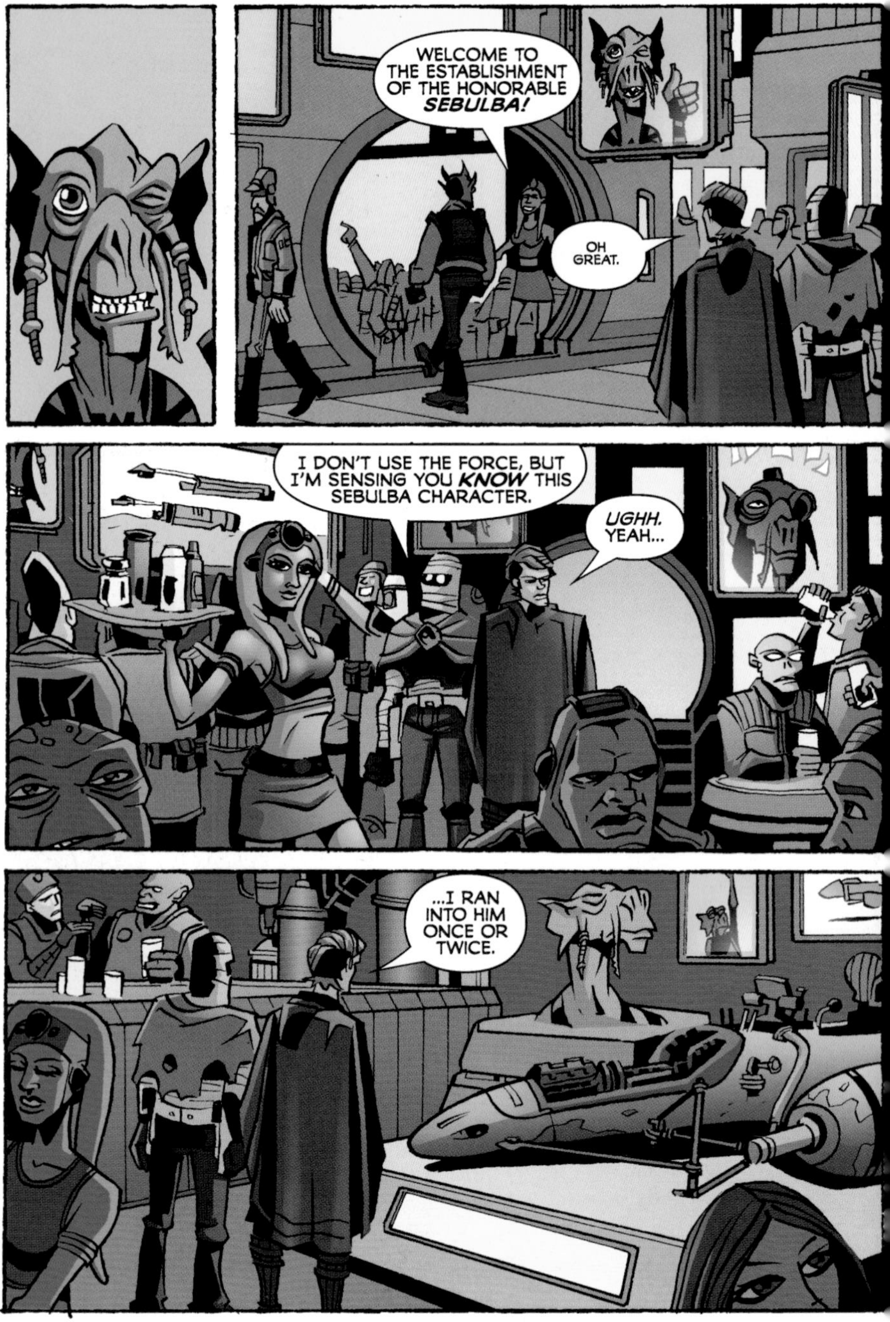
WELCOME TO THE ESTABLISHMENT OF THE HONORABLE *SEBULBA!*
OH GREAT.
I DON'T USE THE FORCE, BUT I'M SENSING YOU *KNOW* THIS SEBULBA CHARACTER.
UGHH. YEAH...
...I RAN INTO HIM ONCE OR TWICE.

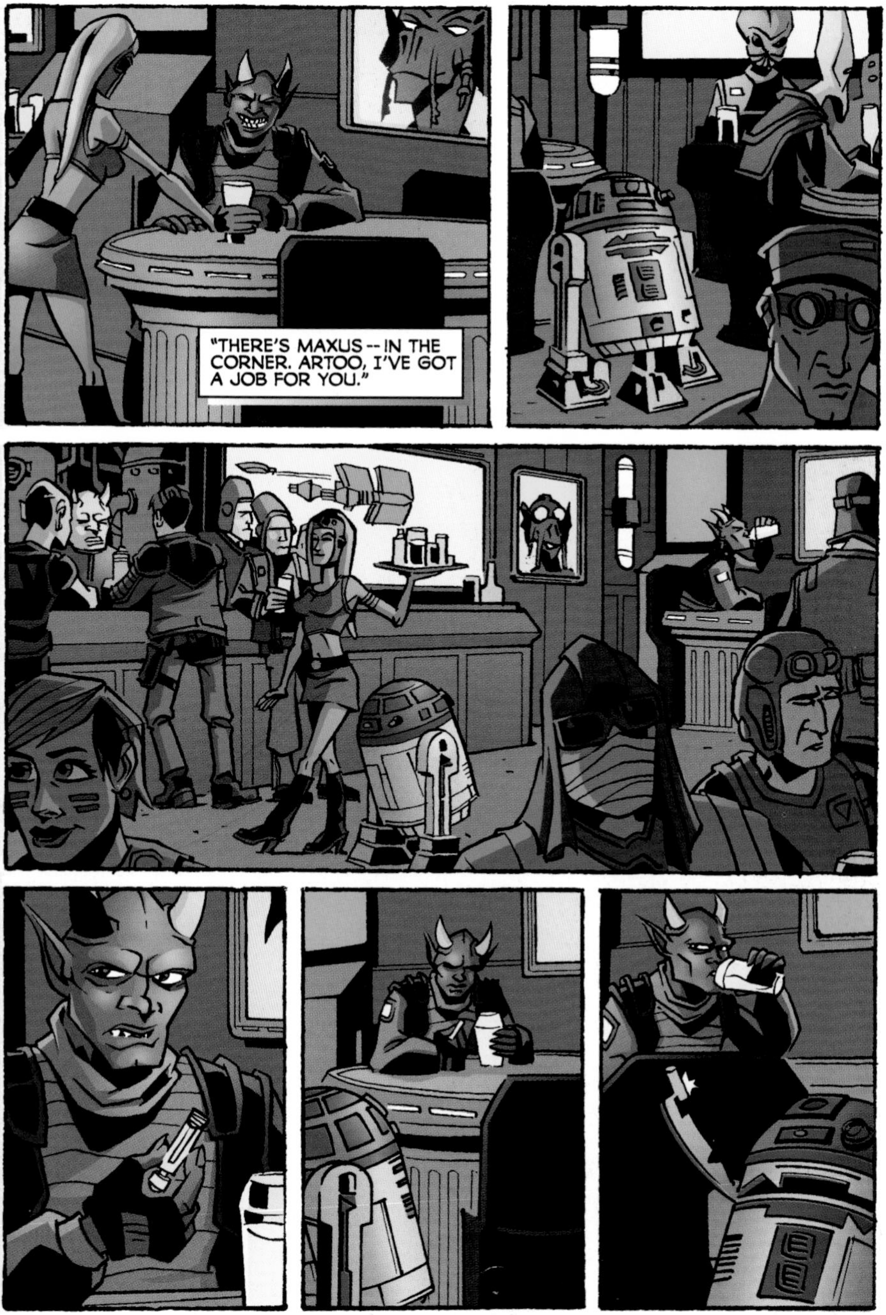
"THERE'S MAXUS -- IN THE CORNER. ARTOO, I'VE GOT A JOB FOR YOU."

AGENT SIXTEEN, HAVE YOU TAKEN POSSESSION OF THE REPUBLIC'S DATA FILE?

I HAVE IT, DOOKU, BUT I'M AFRAID YOUR COURIER, MESSO, MET WITH A MYSTERIOUS ACCIDENT.

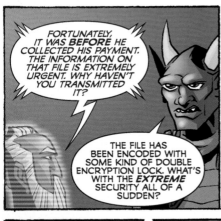

FORTUNATELY, IT WAS **BEFORE** HE COLLECTED HIS PAYMENT. THE INFORMATION ON THAT FILE IS EXTREMELY URGENT. WHY HAVEN'T YOU TRANSMITTED IT?

THE FILE HAS BEEN ENCODED WITH SOME KIND OF DOUBLE ENCRYPTION LOCK. WHAT'S WITH THE **EXTREME** SECURITY ALL OF A SUDDEN?

THE JEDI HAVE BECOME AWARE OF OUR INTELLIGENCE GATHERING OPERATION.

THE **JEDI?!** YOU PROMISED WE WOULDN'T HAVE TO WORRY ABOUT THEM!

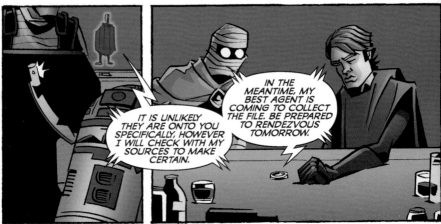

IT IS UNLIKELY THEY ARE ONTO YOU SPECIFICALLY, HOWEVER I WILL CHECK WITH MY SOURCES TO MAKE CERTAIN.

IN THE MEANTIME, MY BEST AGENT IS COMING TO COLLECT THE FILE. BE PREPARED TO RENDEZVOUS TOMORROW.

WE'LL BE READY. AND DOOKU, MAKE SURE YOUR AGENT BRINGS OUR PAYOFF. WE'RE NOT DOING THIS FOR NOTHING.

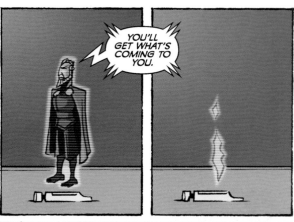

YOU'LL GET WHAT'S COMING TO YOU.

GOOD JOB, ARTOO.

BWOOP!

SO NOW WE WAIT?

AND MAKE SURE NONE OF THEM LEAVES OUR SIGHT.

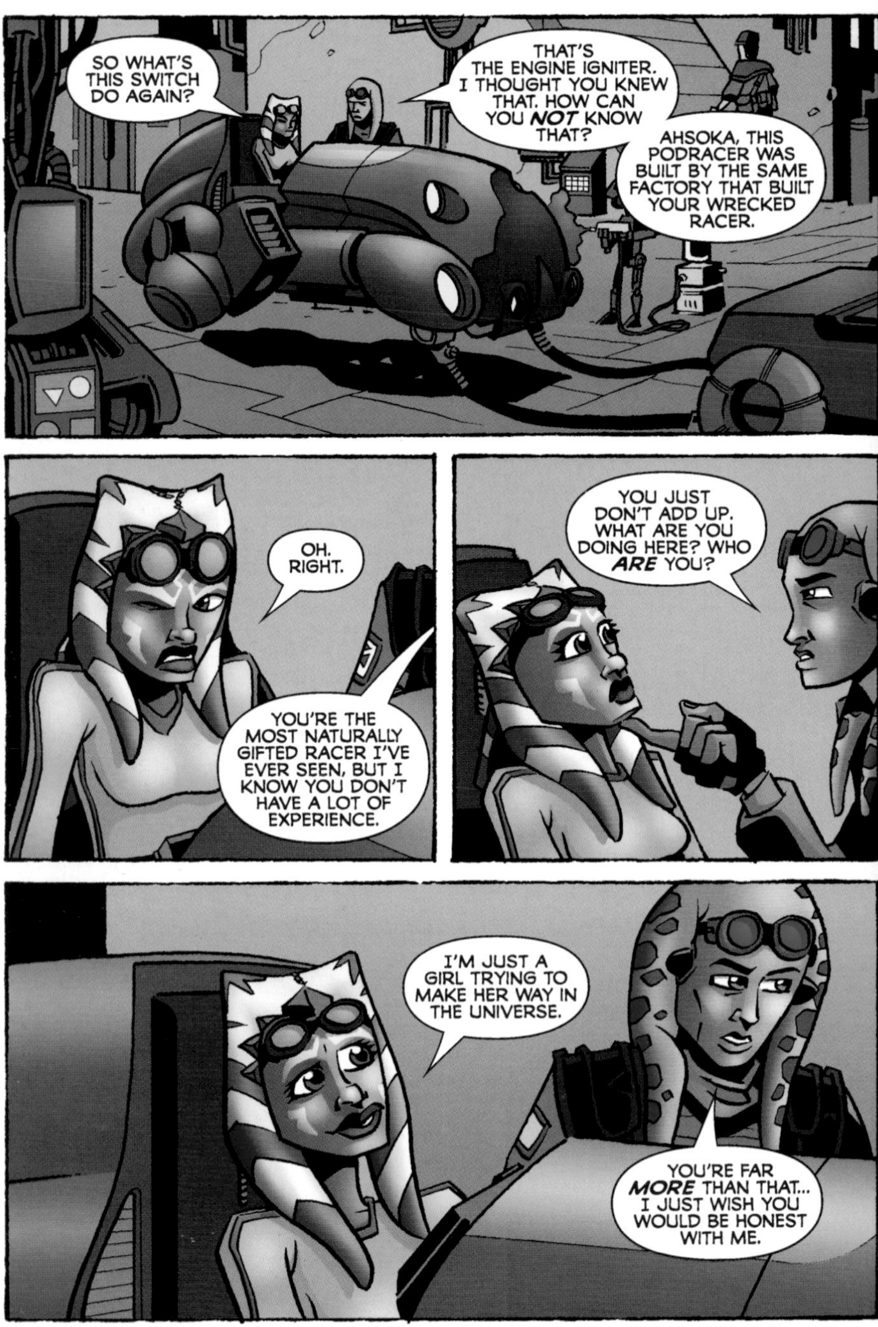
SO WHAT'S THIS SWITCH DO AGAIN?
THAT'S THE ENGINE IGNITER. I THOUGHT YOU KNEW THAT. HOW CAN YOU *NOT* KNOW THAT?
AHSOKA, THIS PODRACER WAS BUILT BY THE SAME FACTORY THAT BUILT YOUR WRECKED RACER.
OH. RIGHT.
YOU'RE THE MOST NATURALLY GIFTED RACER I'VE EVER SEEN, BUT I KNOW YOU DON'T HAVE A LOT OF EXPERIENCE.
YOU JUST DON'T ADD UP. WHAT ARE YOU DOING HERE? WHO *ARE* YOU?
I'M JUST A GIRL TRYING TO MAKE HER WAY IN THE UNIVERSE.
YOU'RE FAR *MORE* THAN THAT... I JUST WISH YOU WOULD BE HONEST WITH ME.

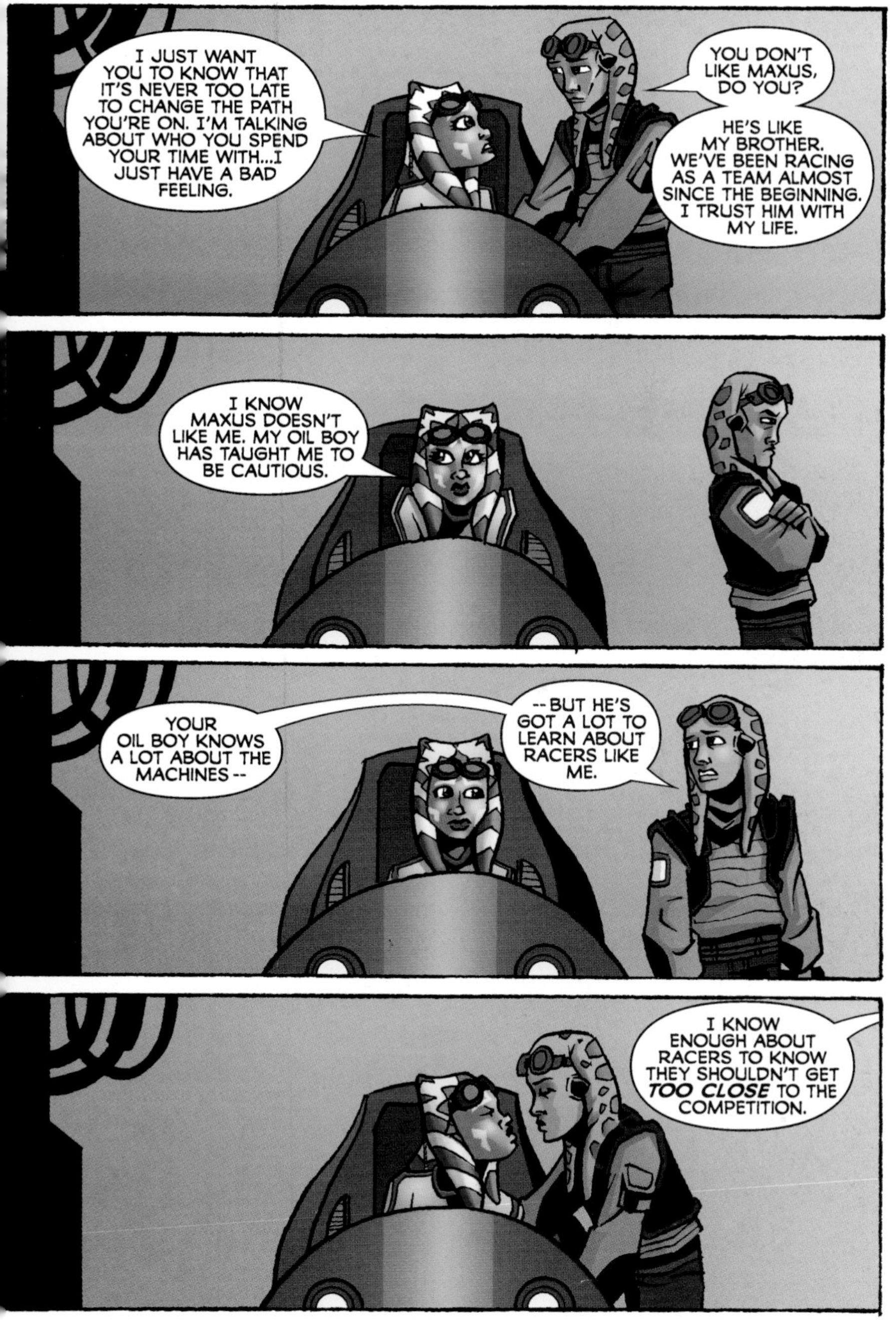
I JUST WANT YOU TO KNOW THAT IT'S NEVER TOO LATE TO CHANGE THE PATH YOU'RE ON. I'M TALKING ABOUT WHO YOU SPEND YOUR TIME WITH...I JUST HAVE A BAD FEELING.
YOU DON'T LIKE MAXUS, DO YOU?
HE'S LIKE MY BROTHER. WE'VE BEEN RACING AS A TEAM ALMOST SINCE THE BEGINNING. I TRUST HIM WITH MY LIFE.
I KNOW MAXUS DOESN'T LIKE ME. MY OIL BOY HAS TAUGHT ME TO BE CAUTIOUS.
YOUR OIL BOY KNOWS A LOT ABOUT THE MACHINES --
-- BUT HE'S GOT A LOT TO LEARN ABOUT RACERS LIKE ME.
I KNOW ENOUGH ABOUT RACERS TO KNOW THEY SHOULDN'T GET *TOO CLOSE* TO THE COMPETITION.

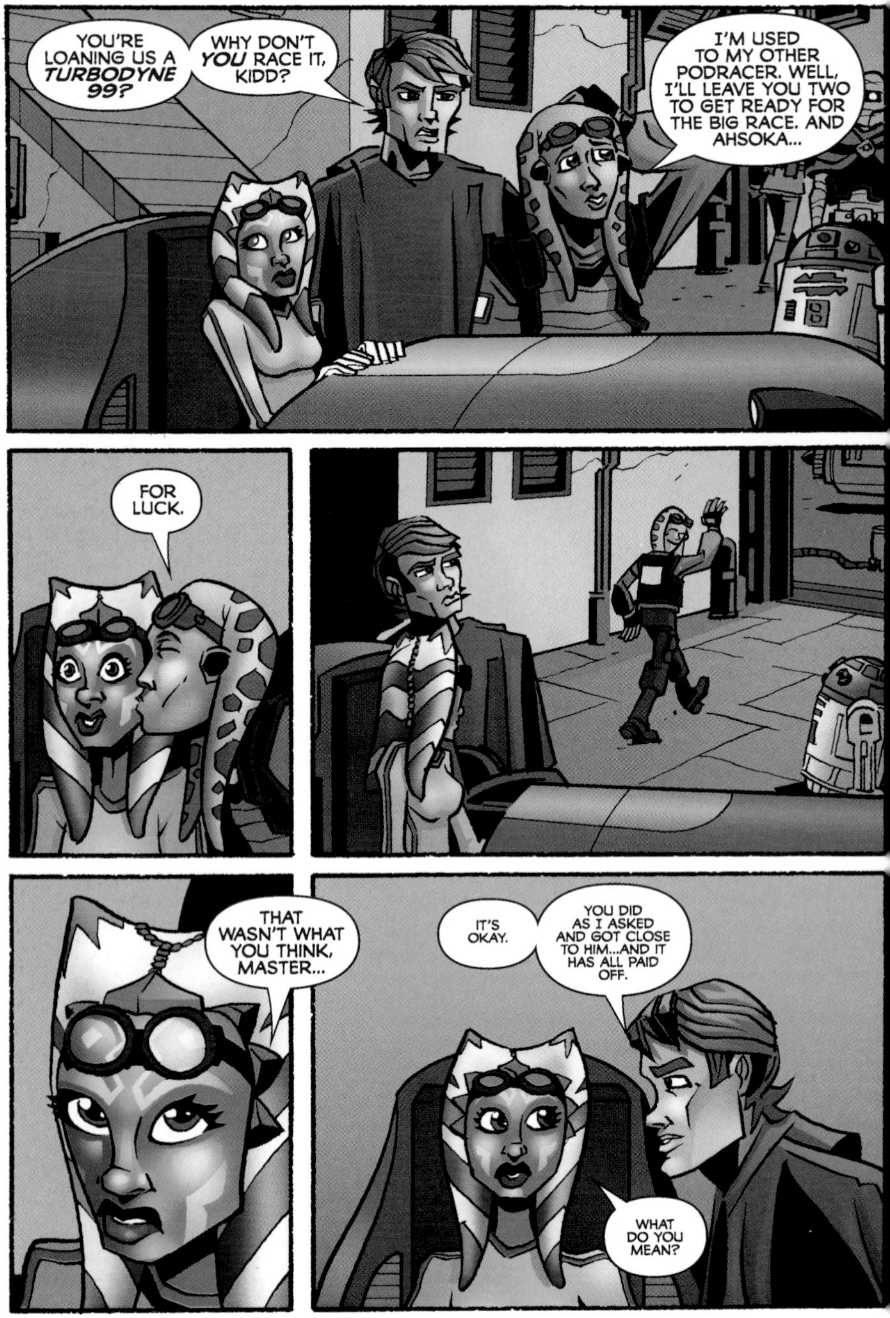
YOU'RE LOANING US A *TURBODYNE 99?*
WHY DON'T *YOU* RACE IT, KIDD?
I'M USED TO MY OTHER PODRACER. WELL, I'LL LEAVE YOU TWO TO GET READY FOR THE BIG RACE. AND AHSOKA...
FOR LUCK.
THAT WASN'T WHAT YOU THINK, MASTER...
IT'S OKAY.
YOU DID AS I ASKED AND GOT CLOSE TO HIM...AND IT HAS ALL PAID OFF.
WHAT DO YOU MEAN?

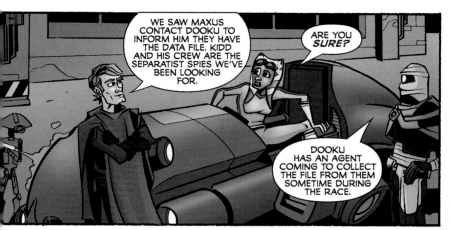

WE SAW MAXUS CONTACT DOOKU TO INFORM HIM THEY HAVE THE DATA FILE. KIDD AND HIS CREW ARE THE SEPARATIST SPIES WE'VE BEEN LOOKING FOR.

ARE YOU *SURE?*

DOOKU HAS AN AGENT COMING TO COLLECT THE FILE FROM THEM SOMETIME DURING THE RACE.

WHICH MEANS *YOU'VE* GOT TO STAY CLOSE TO THEM FOR A LITTLE WHILE LONGER.

I WAS SO *SURE* KIDD WASN'T A SPY.

I'M SORRY. YOUR DESIRE TO THINK THE BEST OF OTHERS DOES YOU CREDIT, BUT I WARNED YOU THIS COULD HAPPEN WHEN YOU LET YOUR FEELINGS GET INVOLVED.

I KNOW YOU'RE RIGHT, MASTER. WE'LL CATCH KIDD AND HIS CREW IN THE ACT AND BRING THEM TO JUSTICE.

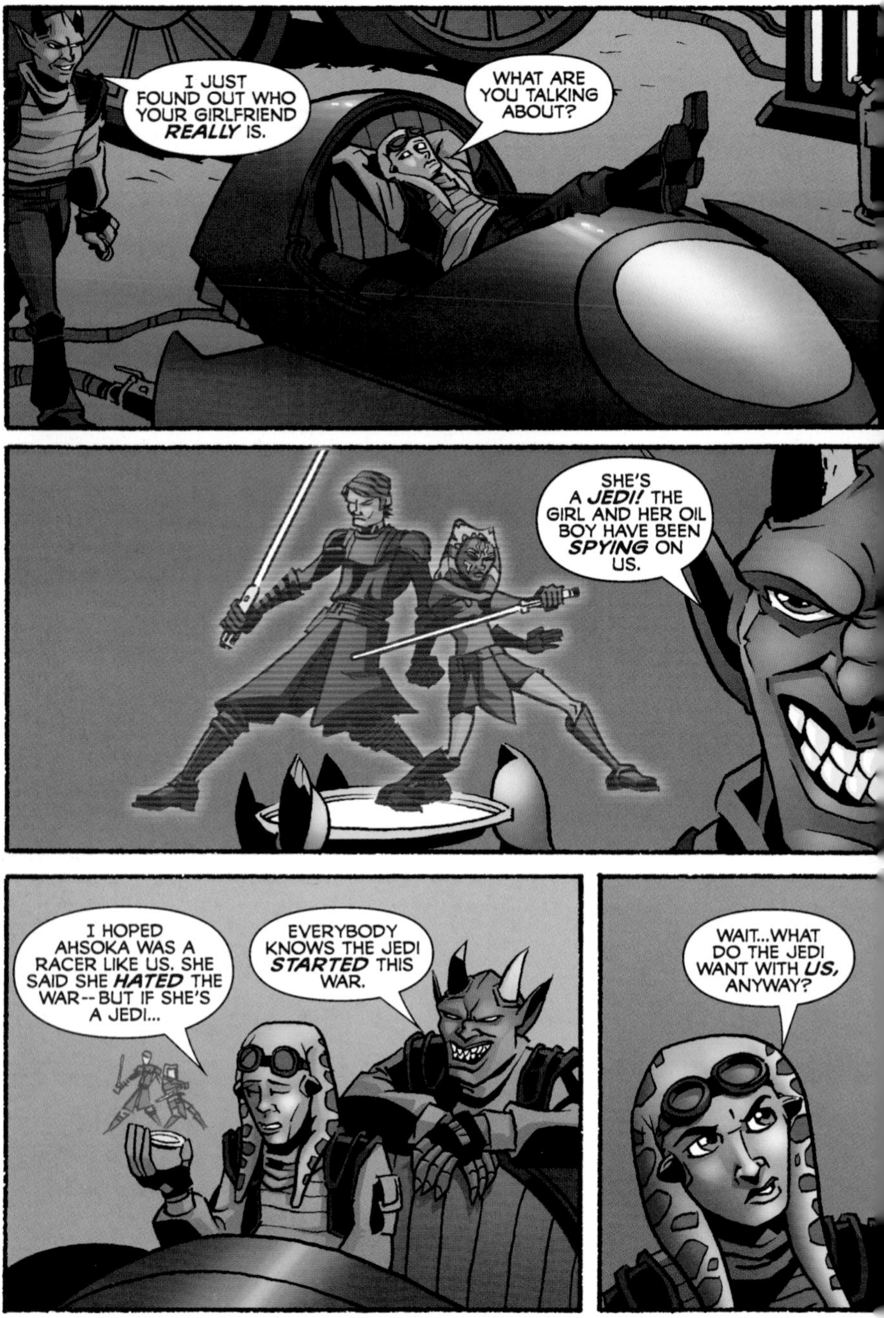
I JUST FOUND OUT WHO YOUR GIRLFRIEND REALLY IS.
WHAT ARE YOU TALKING ABOUT?
SHE'S A JEDI! THE GIRL AND HER OIL BOY HAVE BEEN SPYING ON US.
I HOPED AHSOKA WAS A RACER LIKE US. SHE SAID SHE HATED THE WAR--BUT IF SHE'S A JEDI...
EVERYBODY KNOWS THE JEDI STARTED THIS WAR.
WAIT...WHAT DO THE JEDI WANT WITH US, ANYWAY?

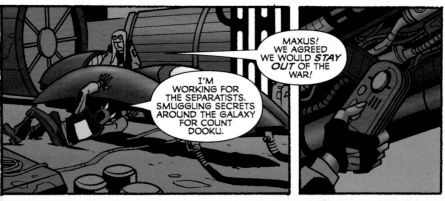

MAXUS! WE AGREED WE WOULD *STAY OUT* OF THE WAR!

I'M WORKING FOR THE SEPARATISTS. SMUGGLING SECRETS AROUND THE GALAXY FOR COUNT DOOKU.

THAT WAS *YOUR* IDEA, KIDD. I COULDN'T PASS UP THE WEALTH...AND THE PROMISE OF POWER IN THE FUTURE. I DON'T WANT TO HAVE TO RACE FOREVER.

THE POINT IS IF THE JEDI CATCH US, WE'LL ALL GO TO THE REPUBLIC STOCKADE.

BUT I'M *INNOCENT.*

WHO'S GOING TO *BELIEVE* YOU? THIS IS *YOUR* RACING TEAM. NOW WILL YOU DO WHAT I SAY--OR WILL YOU GO TO *PRISON?*

WHAT DO YOU WANT ME TO DO?

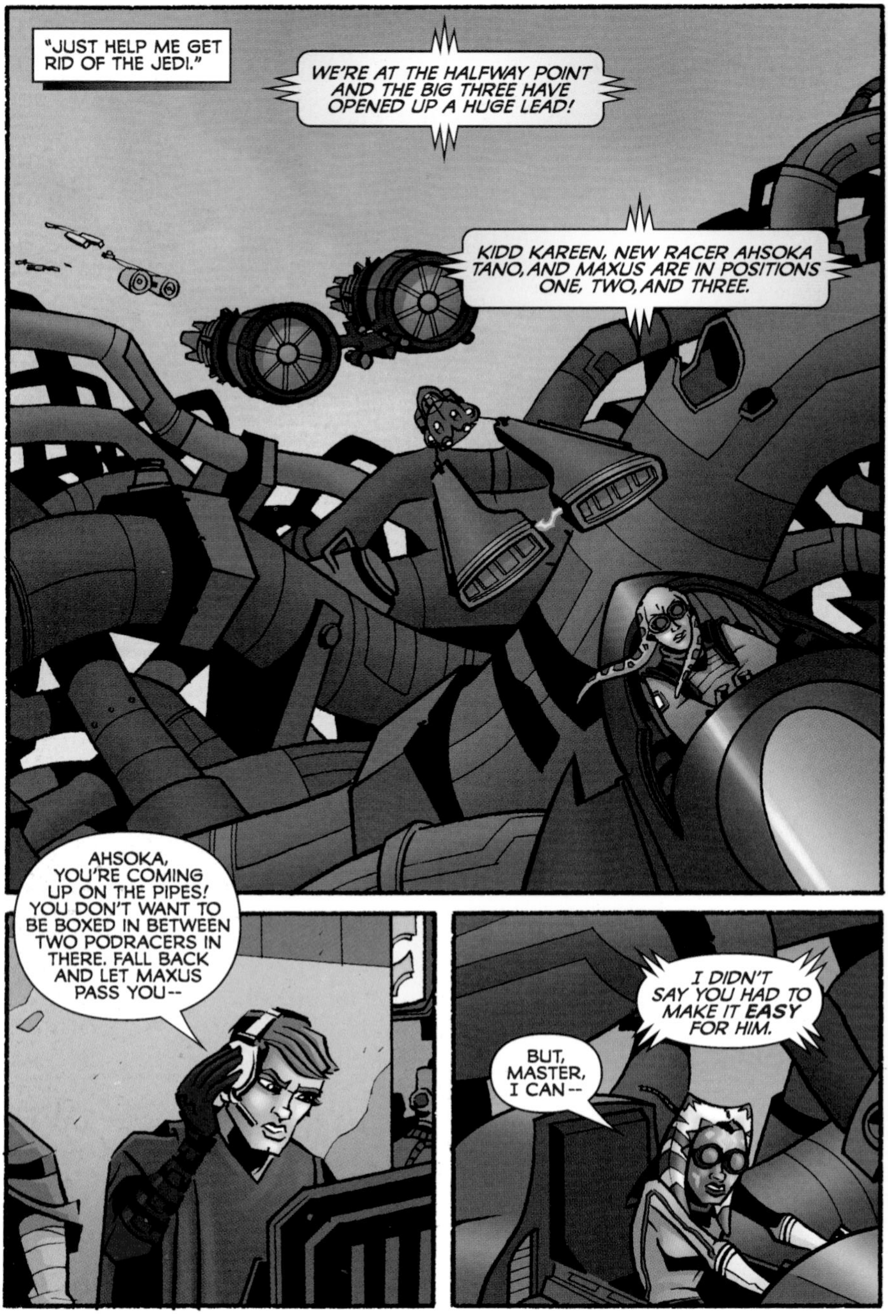
"JUST HELP ME GET RID OF THE JEDI."
WE'RE AT THE HALFWAY POINT AND THE BIG THREE HAVE OPENED UP A HUGE LEAD!
KIDD KAREEN, NEW RACER AHSOKA TANO, AND MAXUS ARE IN POSITIONS ONE, TWO, AND THREE.
AHSOKA, YOU'RE COMING UP ON THE PIPES! YOU DON'T WANT TO BE BOXED IN BETWEEN TWO PODRACERS IN THERE. FALL BACK AND LET MAXUS PASS YOU--
BUT, MASTER, I CAN--
I DIDN'T SAY YOU HAD TO MAKE IT EASY FOR HIM.

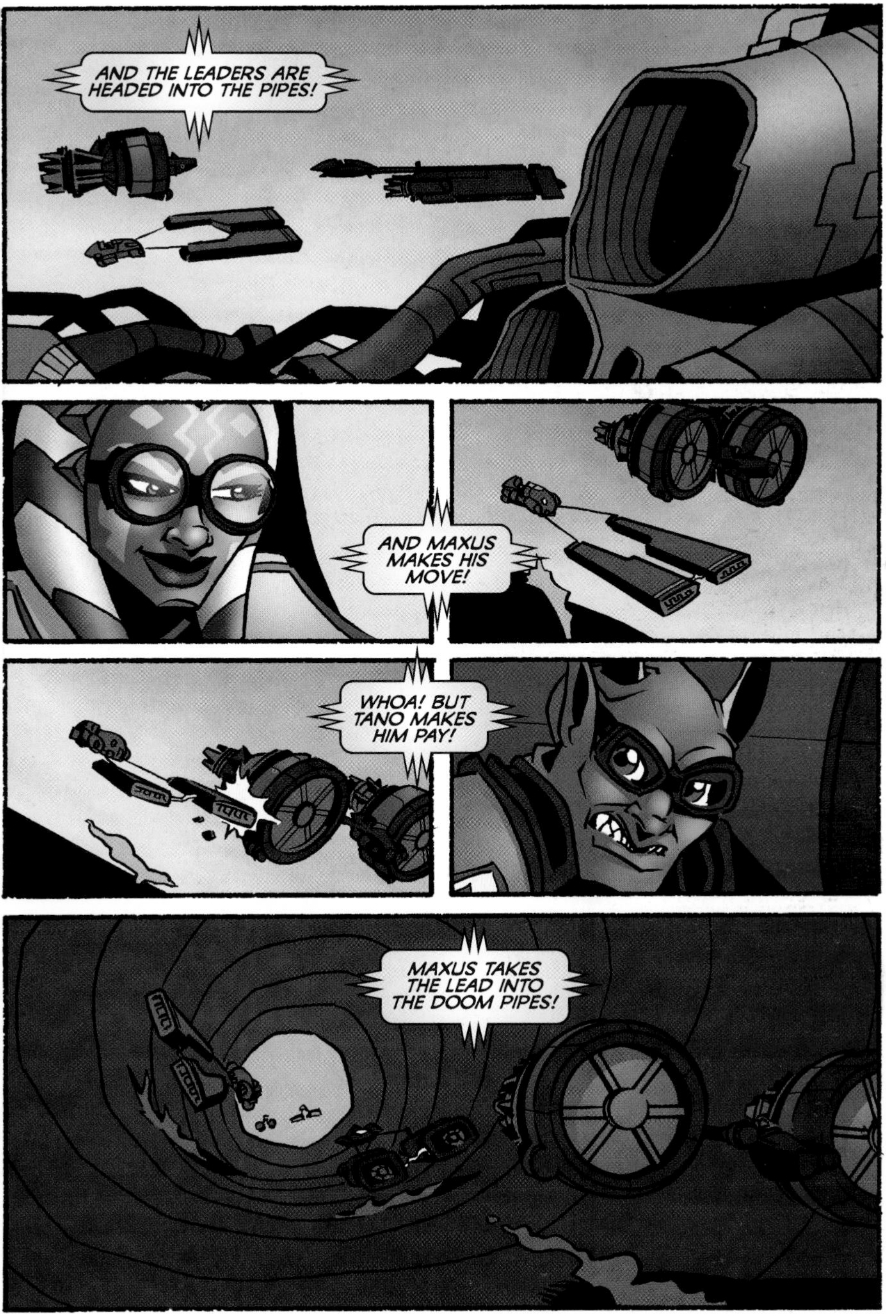
AND THE LEADERS ARE HEADED INTO THE PIPES!
AND MAXUS MAKES HIS MOVE!
WHOA! BUT TANO MAKES HIM PAY!
MAXUS TAKES THE LEAD INTO THE DOOM PIPES!

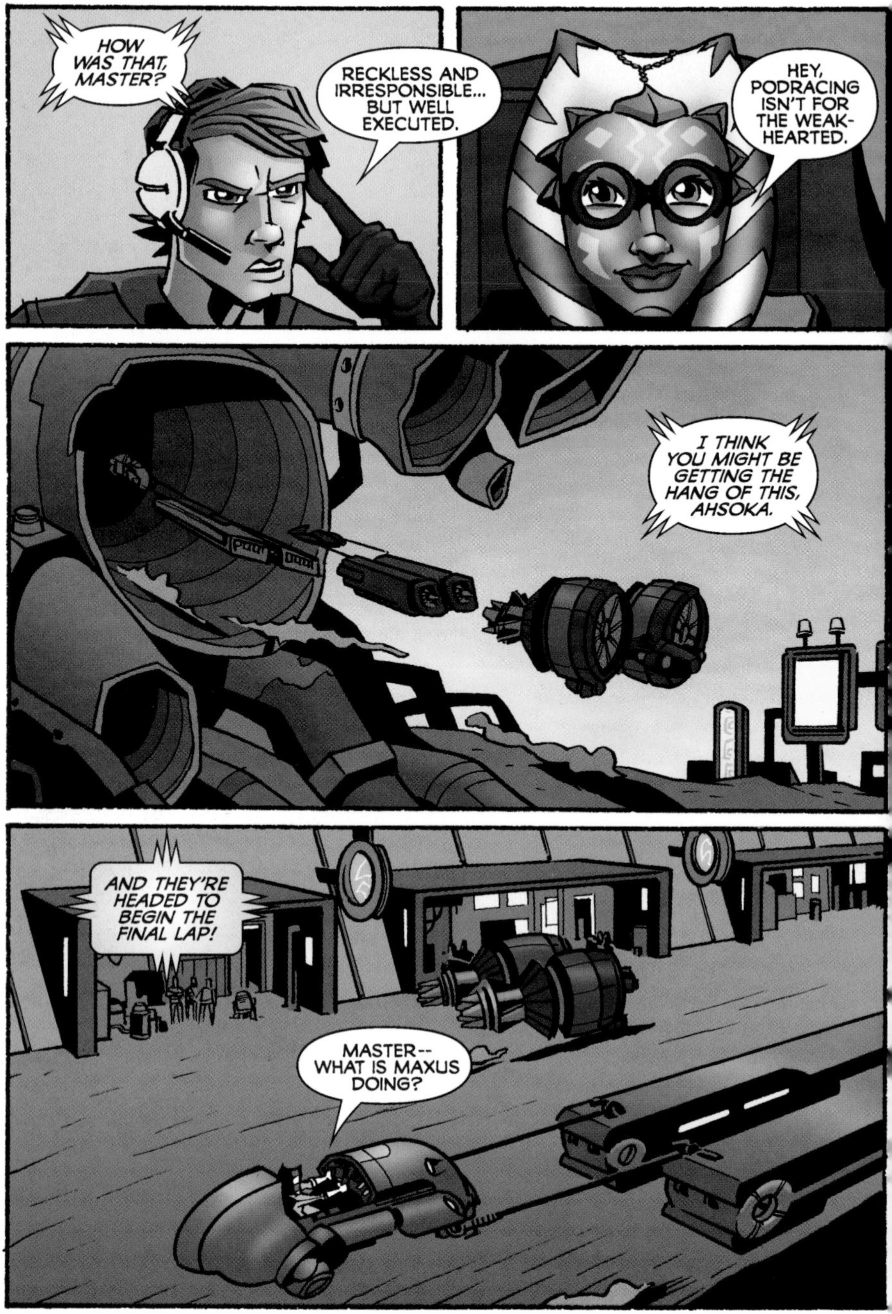
HOW WAS THAT, MASTER?
RECKLESS AND IRRESPONSIBLE... BUT WELL EXECUTED.
HEY, PODRACING ISN'T FOR THE WEAK-HEARTED.
I THINK YOU MIGHT BE GETTING THE HANG OF THIS, AHSOKA.
AND THEY'RE HEADED TO BEGIN THE FINAL LAP!
MASTER-- WHAT IS MAXUS DOING?

I'M NOT SURE...

A CURIOUS DECISION HERE -- MAXUS HAS DROPPED INTO THE PITS **BEFORE** THE FINAL LAP.

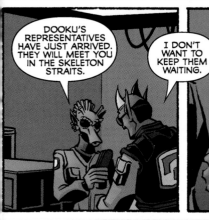

DOOKU'S REPRESENTATIVES HAVE JUST ARRIVED. THEY WILL MEET YOU IN THE SKELETON STRAITS.

I DON'T WANT TO KEEP THEM WAITING.

THE *DATA FILE!*

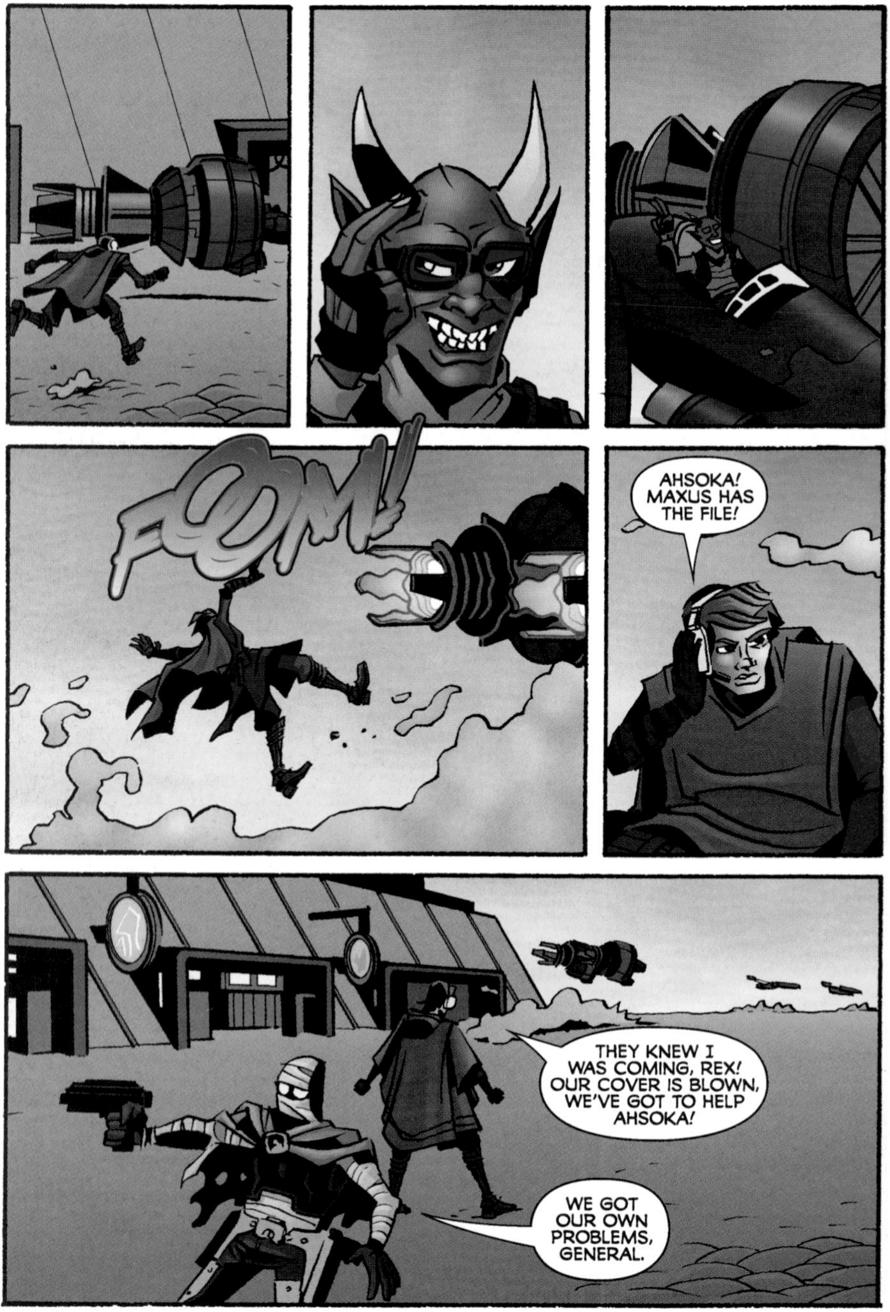
FOOM!
AHSOKA! MAXUS HAS THE FILE!
THEY KNEW I WAS COMING, REX! OUR COVER IS BLOWN, WE'VE GOT TO HELP AHSOKA!
WE GOT OUR OWN PROBLEMS, GENERAL.

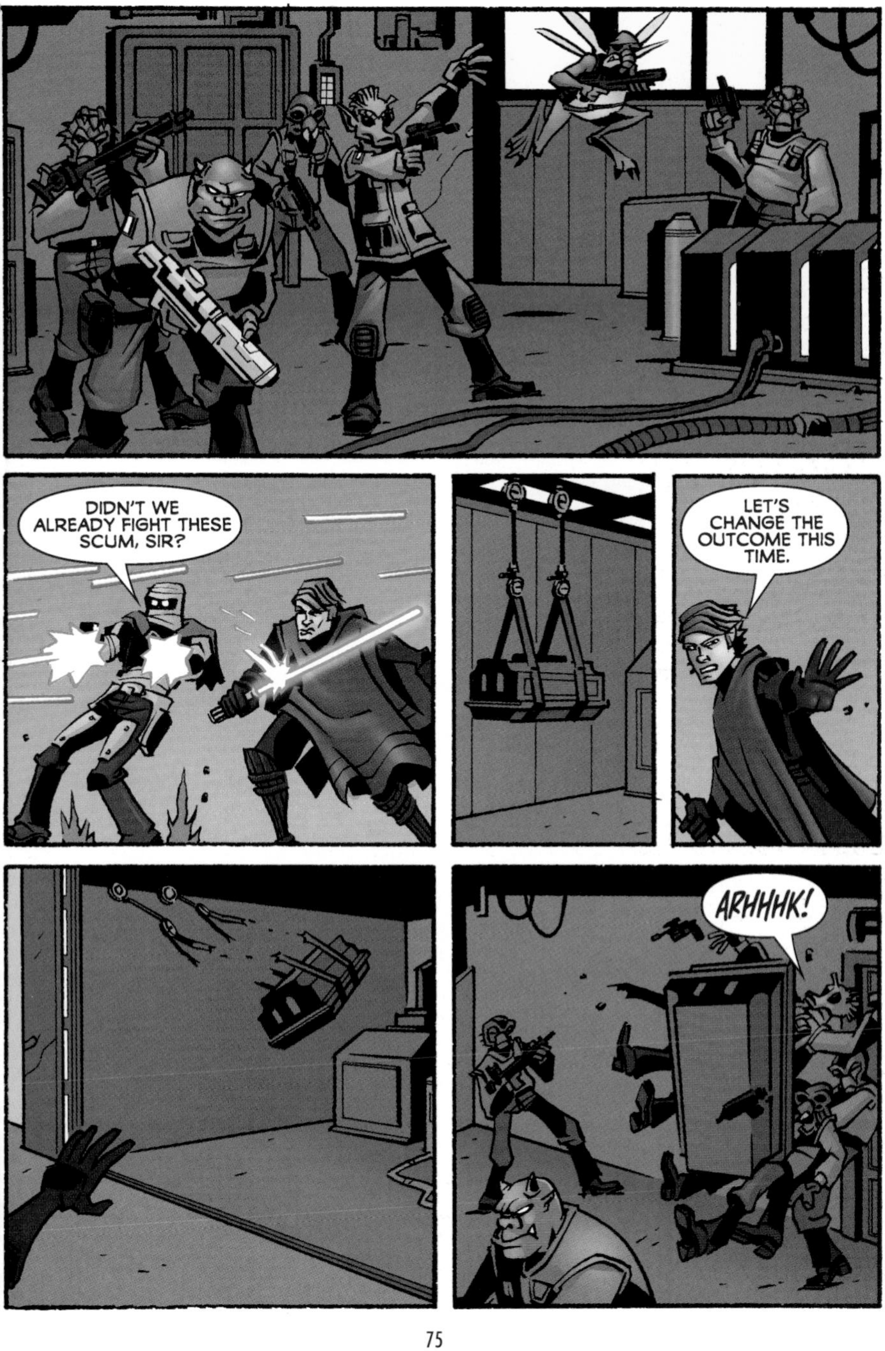
DIDN'T WE ALREADY FIGHT THESE SCUM, SIR?
LET'S CHANGE THE OUTCOME THIS TIME.
ARHHHK!

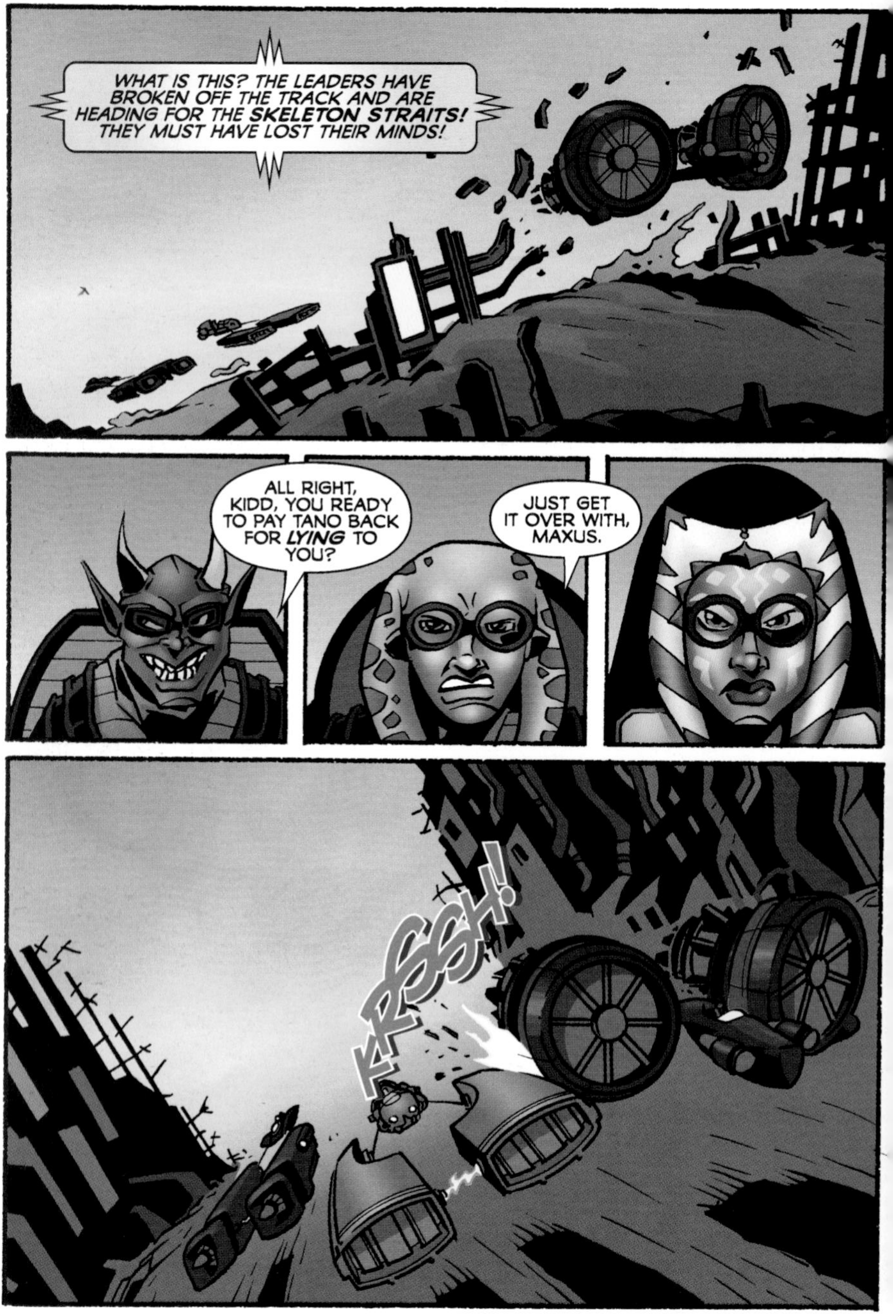
WHAT IS THIS? THE LEADERS HAVE BROKEN OFF THE TRACK AND ARE HEADING FOR THE SKELETON STRAITS! THEY MUST HAVE LOST THEIR MINDS!
ALL RIGHT, KIDD, YOU READY TO PAY TANO BACK FOR LYING TO YOU?
JUST GET IT OVER WITH, MAXUS.
KRSSH!

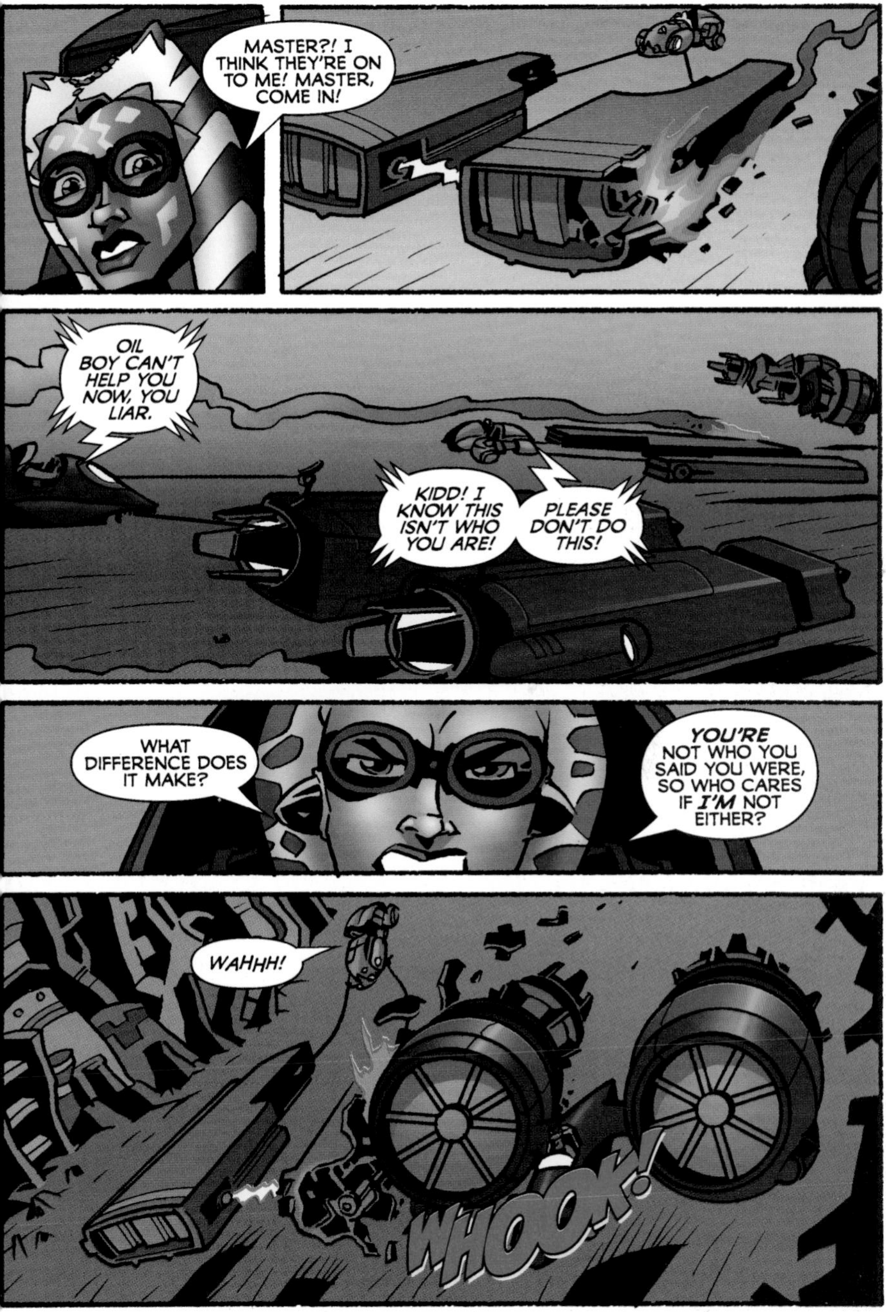
MASTER?! I THINK THEY'RE ON TO ME! MASTER, COME IN!
OIL BOY CAN'T HELP YOU NOW, YOU LIAR.
KIDD! I KNOW THIS ISN'T WHO YOU ARE!
PLEASE DON'T DO THIS!
WHAT DIFFERENCE DOES IT MAKE?
YOU'RE NOT WHO YOU SAID YOU WERE, SO WHO CARES IF I'M NOT EITHER?
WAHHH!
WHOOK!

KIDD, I NEED YOUR HELP. IT'S NOT TOO LATE TO CHANGE YOUR PATH!

GET CLEAR, KIDD. I'M GONNA *FINISH* HER!

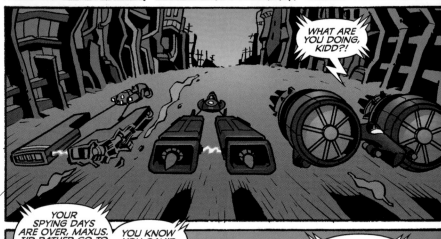

WHAT ARE YOU DOING, KIDD?!

YOUR SPYING DAYS ARE OVER, MAXUS. I'D RATHER GO TO THE STOCKADE FOREVER THAN LET HER GET HURT.

YOU KNOW YOU CAN'T BEAT ME, SO GIVE IT UP.

IF YOU WANT TO SAVE THE JEDI, IT'S YOUR END OF DAYS. I'VE GOT A *DELIVERY* TO MAKE.

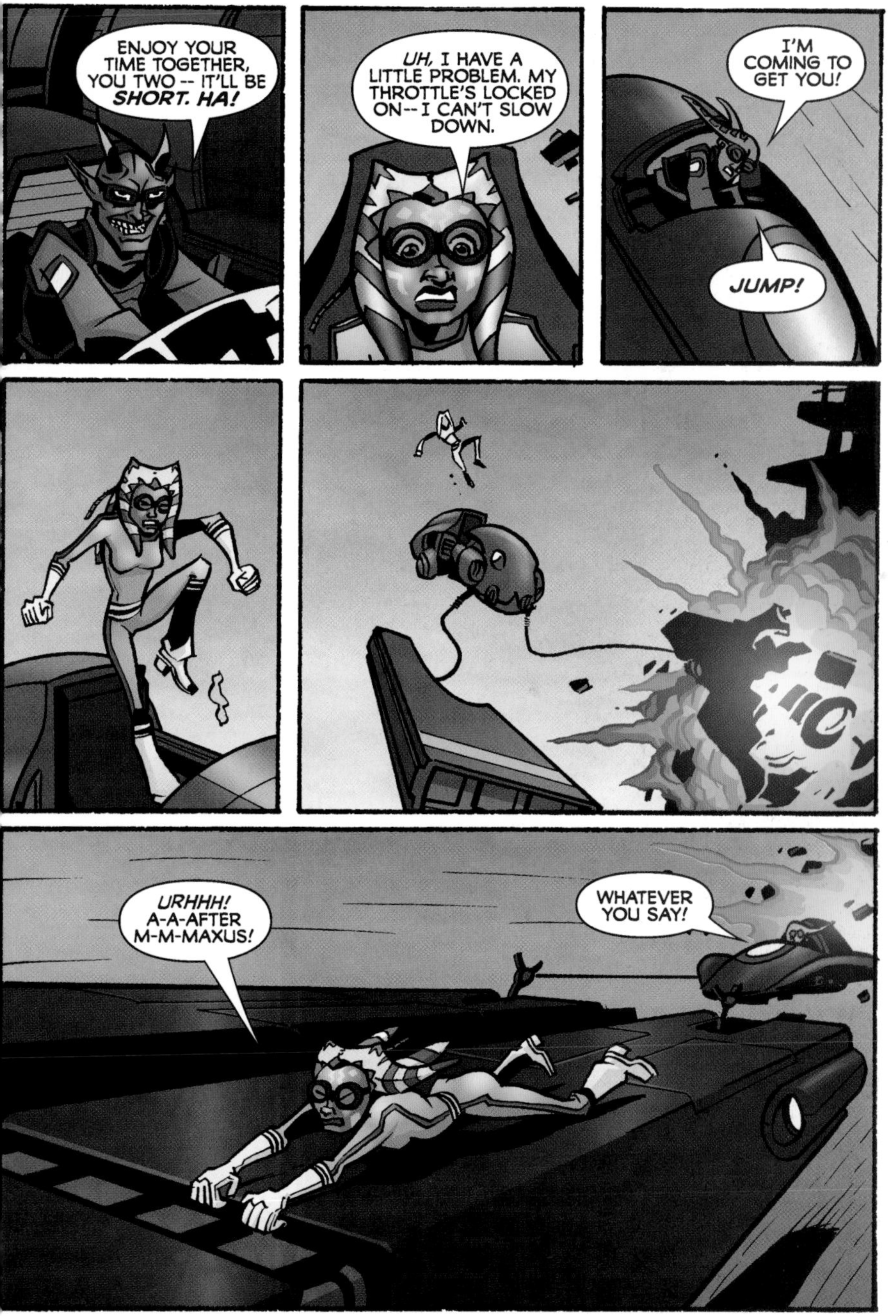
ENJOY YOUR TIME TOGETHER, YOU TWO -- IT'LL BE *SHORT. HA!*
UH, I HAVE A LITTLE PROBLEM. MY THROTTLE'S LOCKED ON-- I CAN'T SLOW DOWN.
I'M COMING TO GET YOU!
JUMP!
URHHH! A-A-AFTER M-M-MAXUS!
WHATEVER YOU SAY!

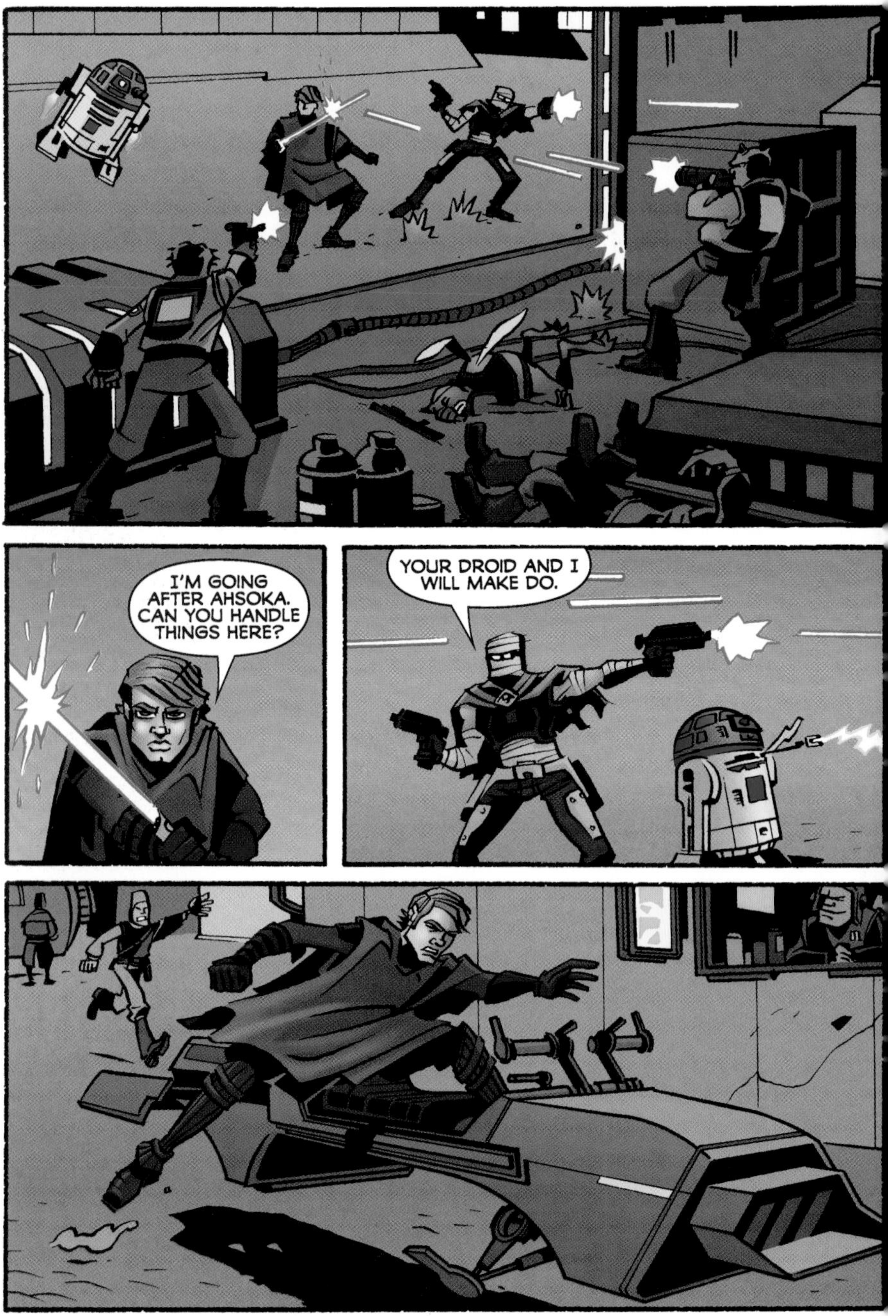
I'M GOING AFTER AHSOKA. CAN YOU HANDLE THINGS HERE?
YOUR DROID AND I WILL MAKE DO.

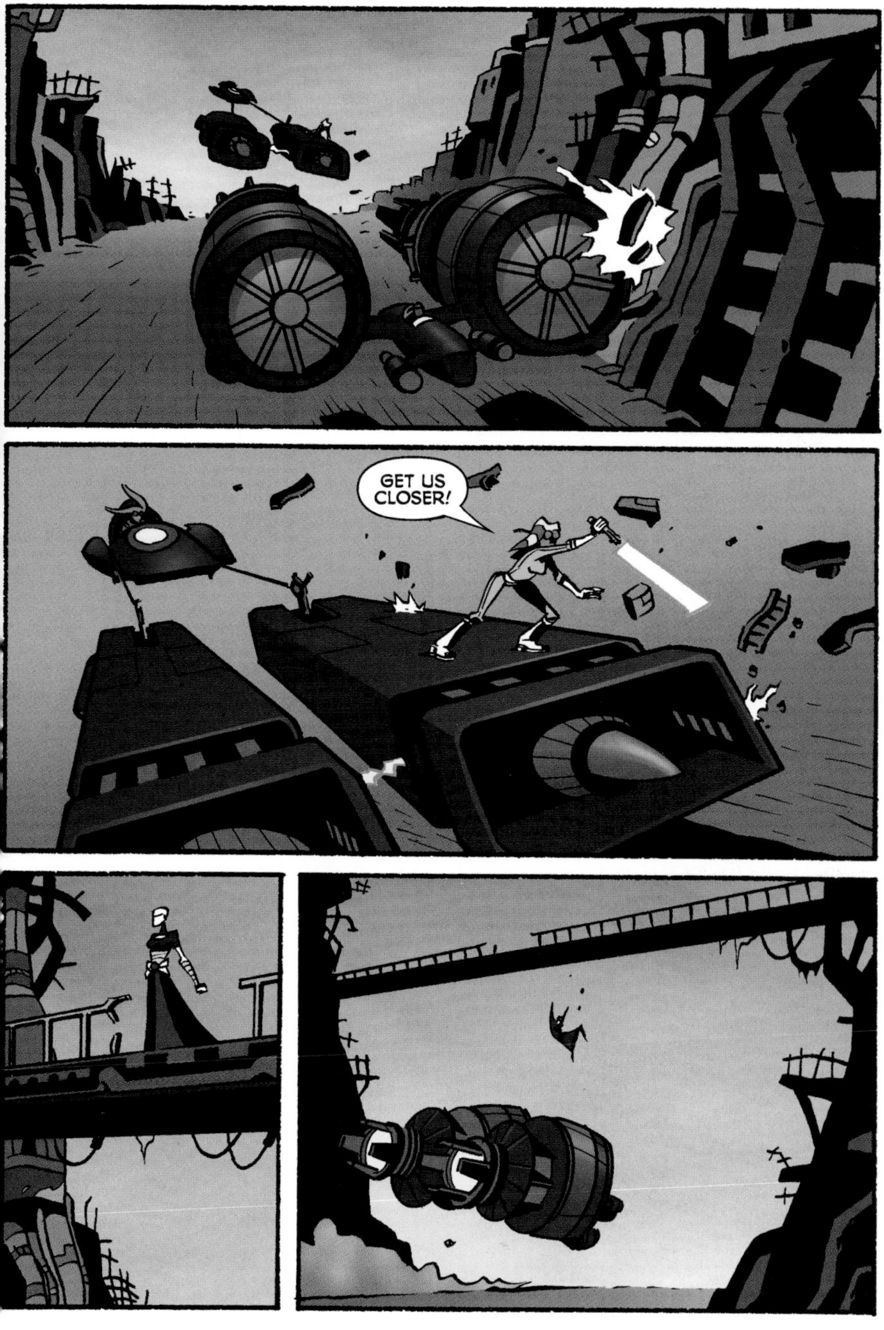
GET US
CLOSER!

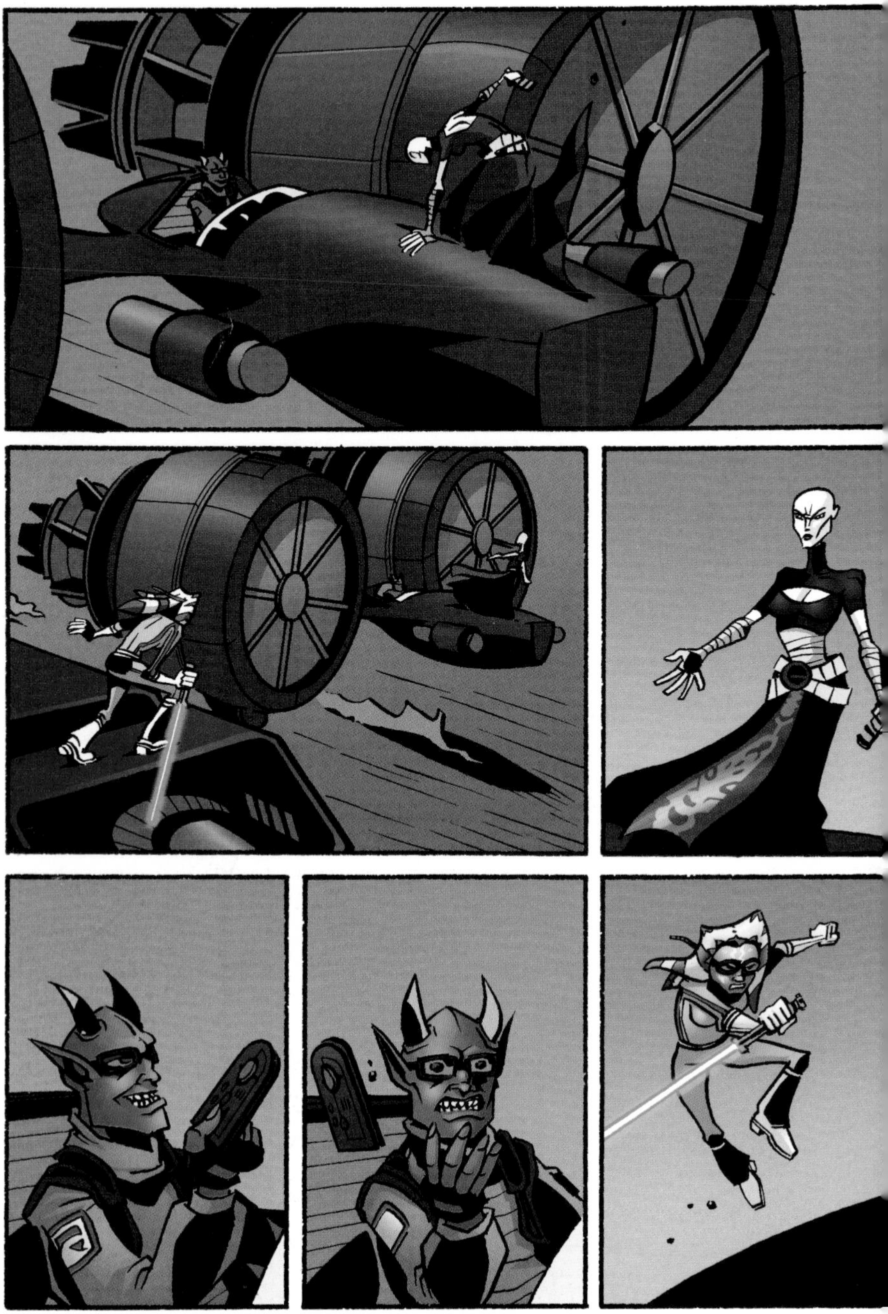

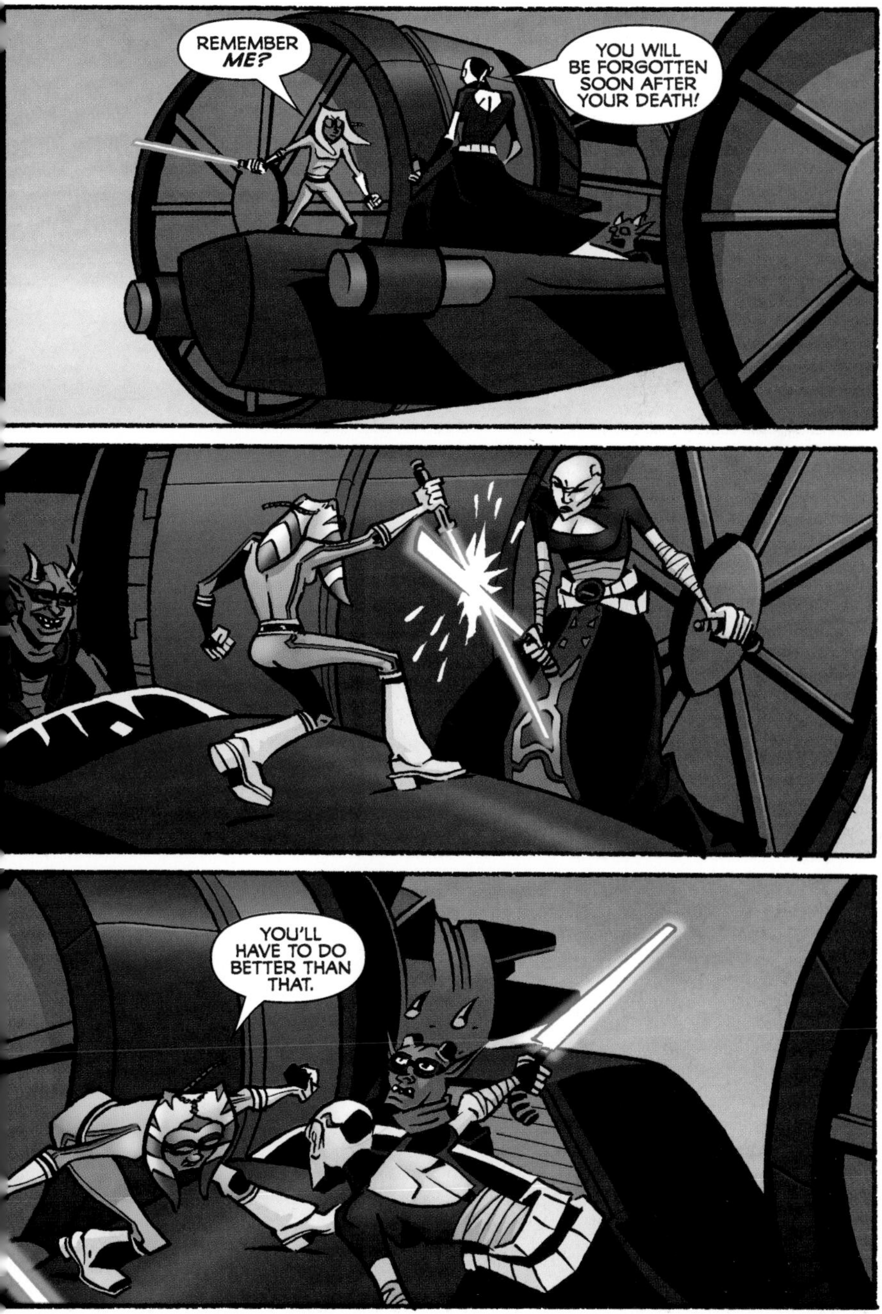
REMEMBER *ME?*
YOU WILL BE FORGOTTEN SOON AFTER YOUR DEATH!
YOU'LL HAVE TO DO BETTER THAN THAT.

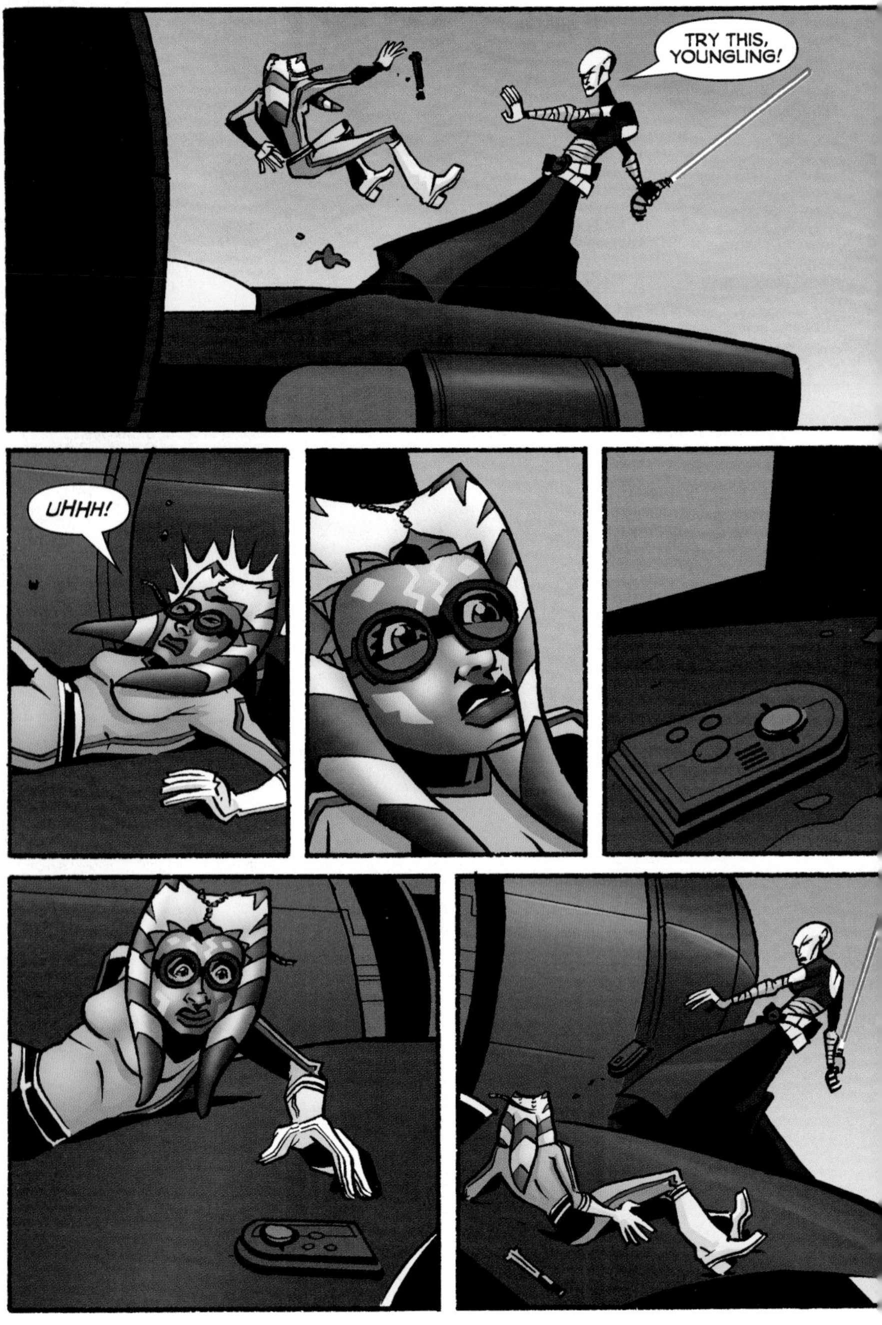
TRY THIS, YOUNGLING!
UHHH!

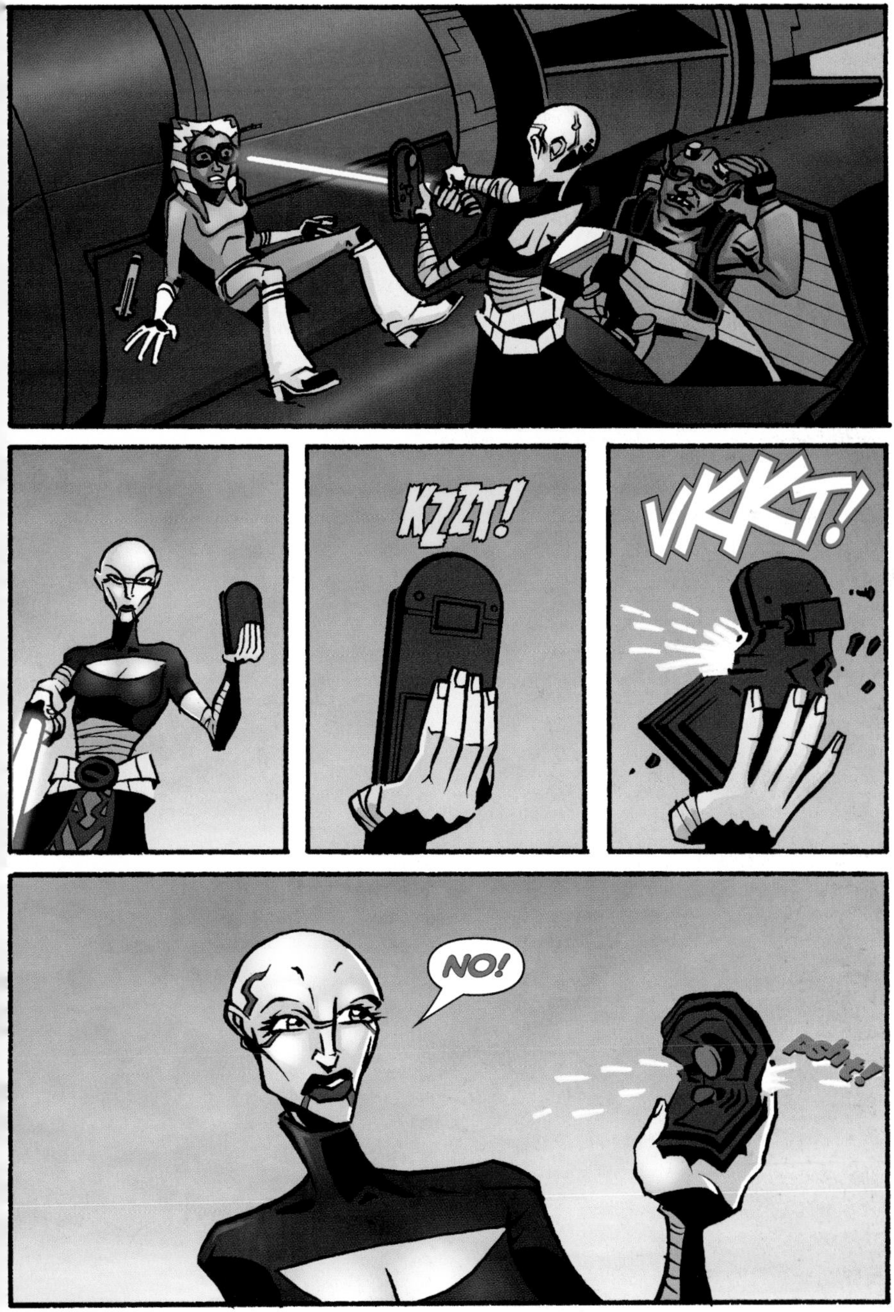
KZZT!
VKKT!
NO!
psht!

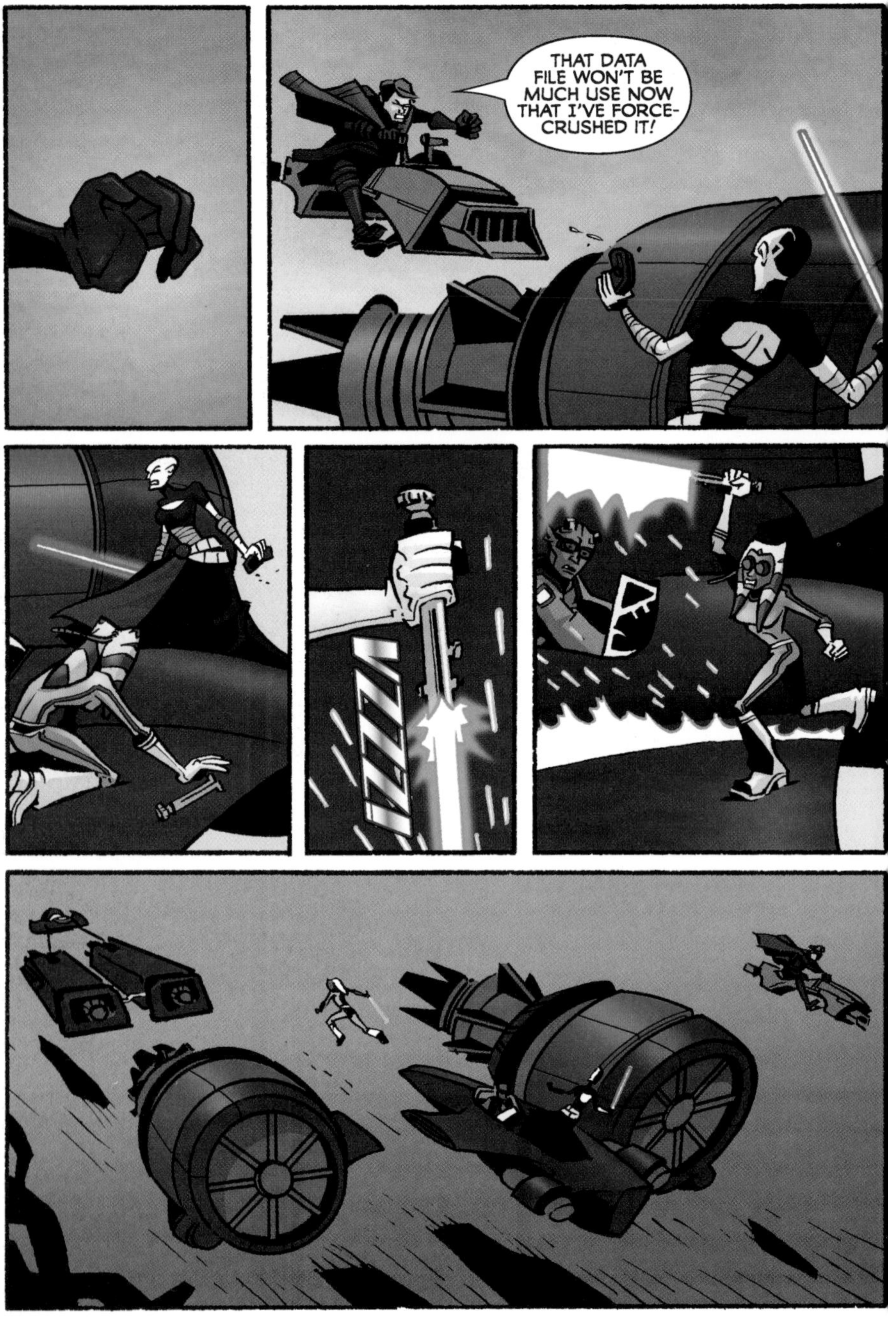
THAT DATA FILE WON'T BE MUCH USE NOW THAT I'VE FORCE-CRUSHED IT!

HELP ME! HELP ME! *HELP ME!*
HELP YOURSELF.

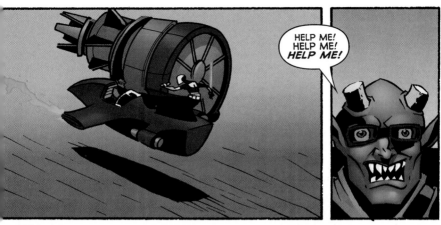

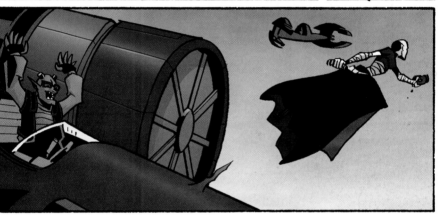

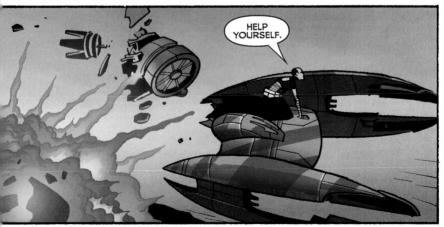

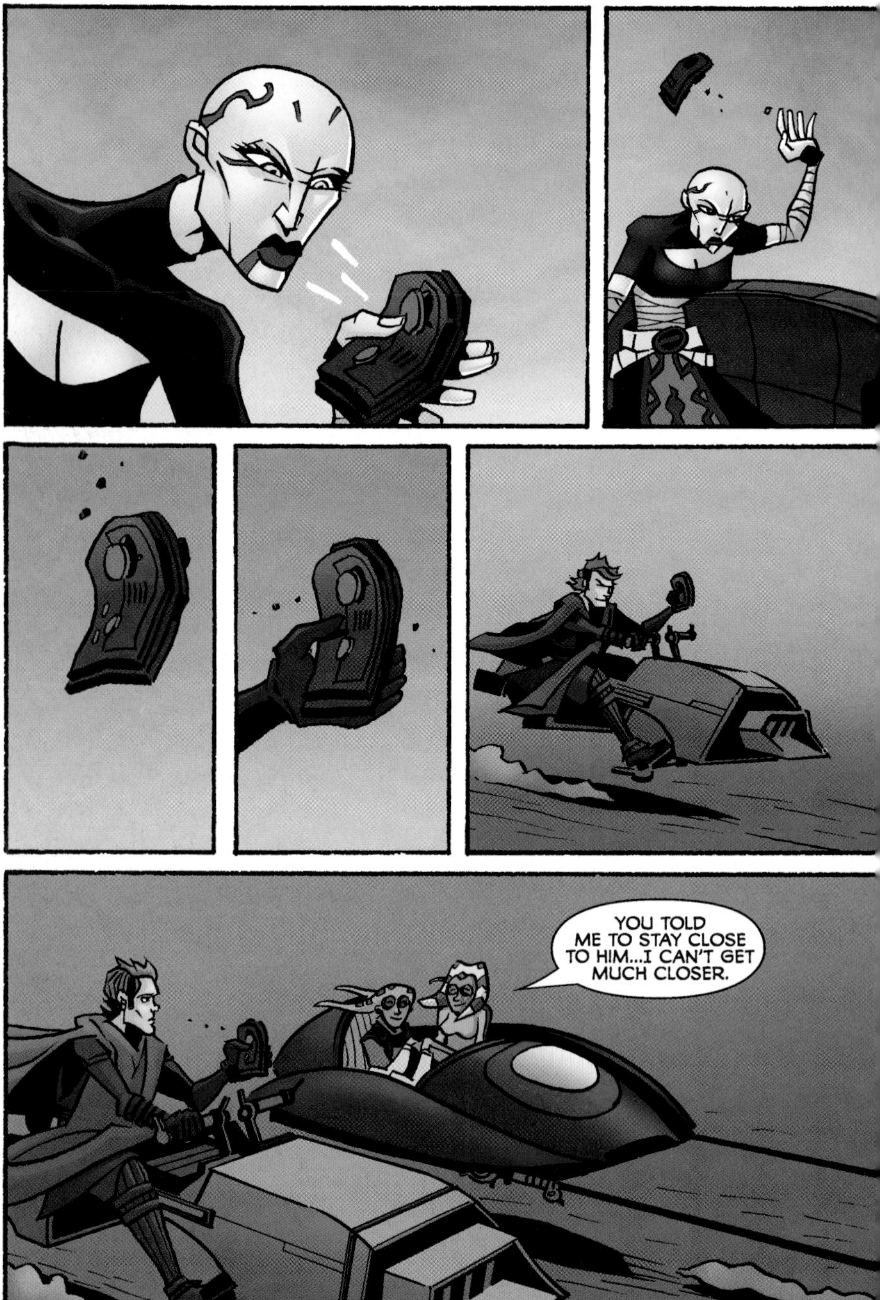
YOU TOLD ME TO STAY CLOSE TO HIM...I CAN'T GET MUCH CLOSER.

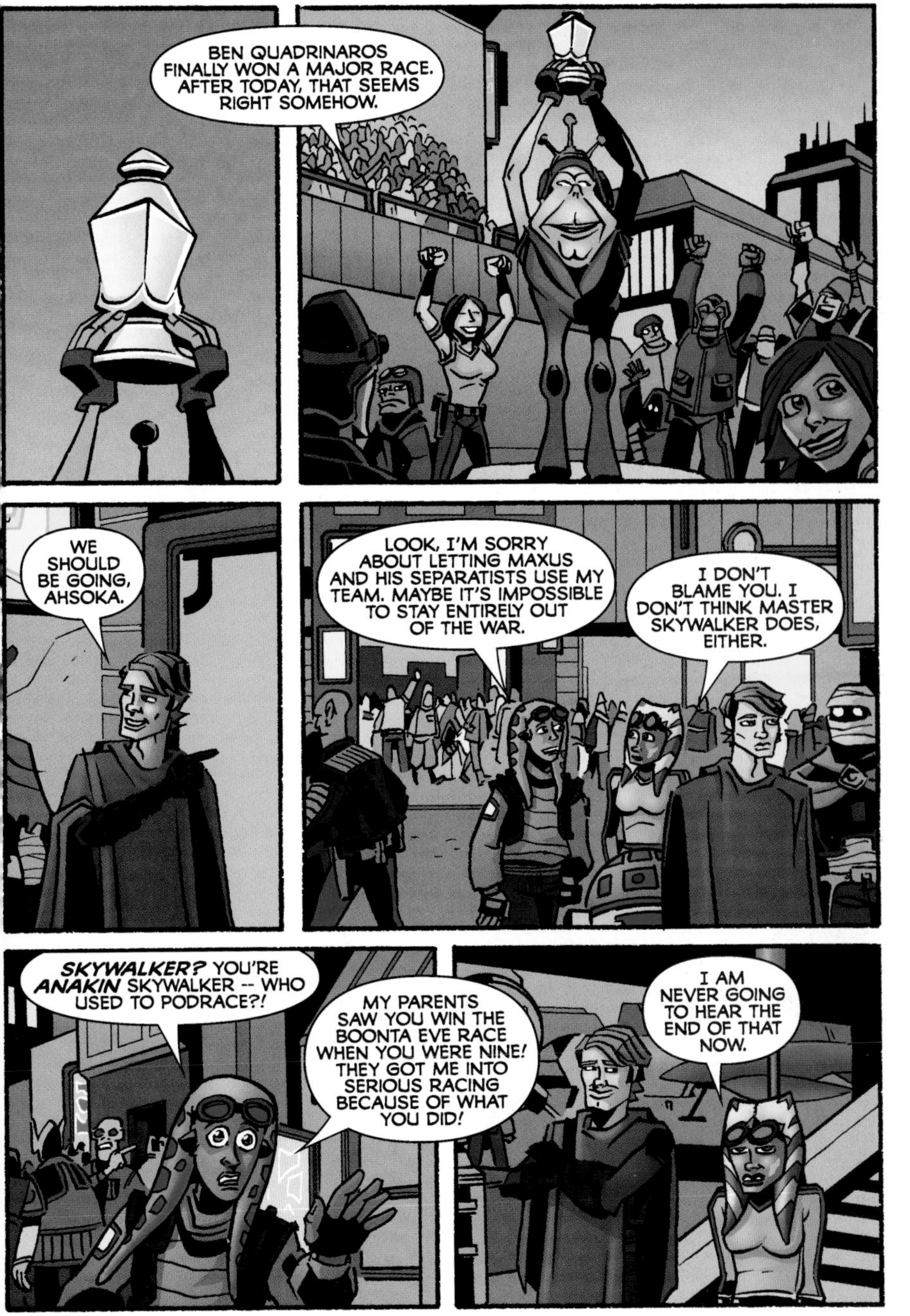

BEN QUADRINAROS FINALLY WON A MAJOR RACE. AFTER TODAY, THAT SEEMS RIGHT SOMEHOW.
WE SHOULD BE GOING, AHSOKA.
LOOK, I'M SORRY ABOUT LETTING MAXUS AND HIS SEPARATISTS USE MY TEAM. MAYBE IT'S IMPOSSIBLE TO STAY ENTIRELY OUT OF THE WAR.
I DON'T BLAME YOU. I DON'T THINK MASTER SKYWALKER DOES, EITHER.
SKYWALKER? YOU'RE ANAKIN SKYWALKER -- WHO USED TO PODRACE?!
MY PARENTS SAW YOU WIN THE BOONTA EVE RACE WHEN YOU WERE NINE! THEY GOT ME INTO SERIOUS RACING BECAUSE OF WHAT YOU DID!
I AM NEVER GOING TO HEAR THE END OF THAT NOW.

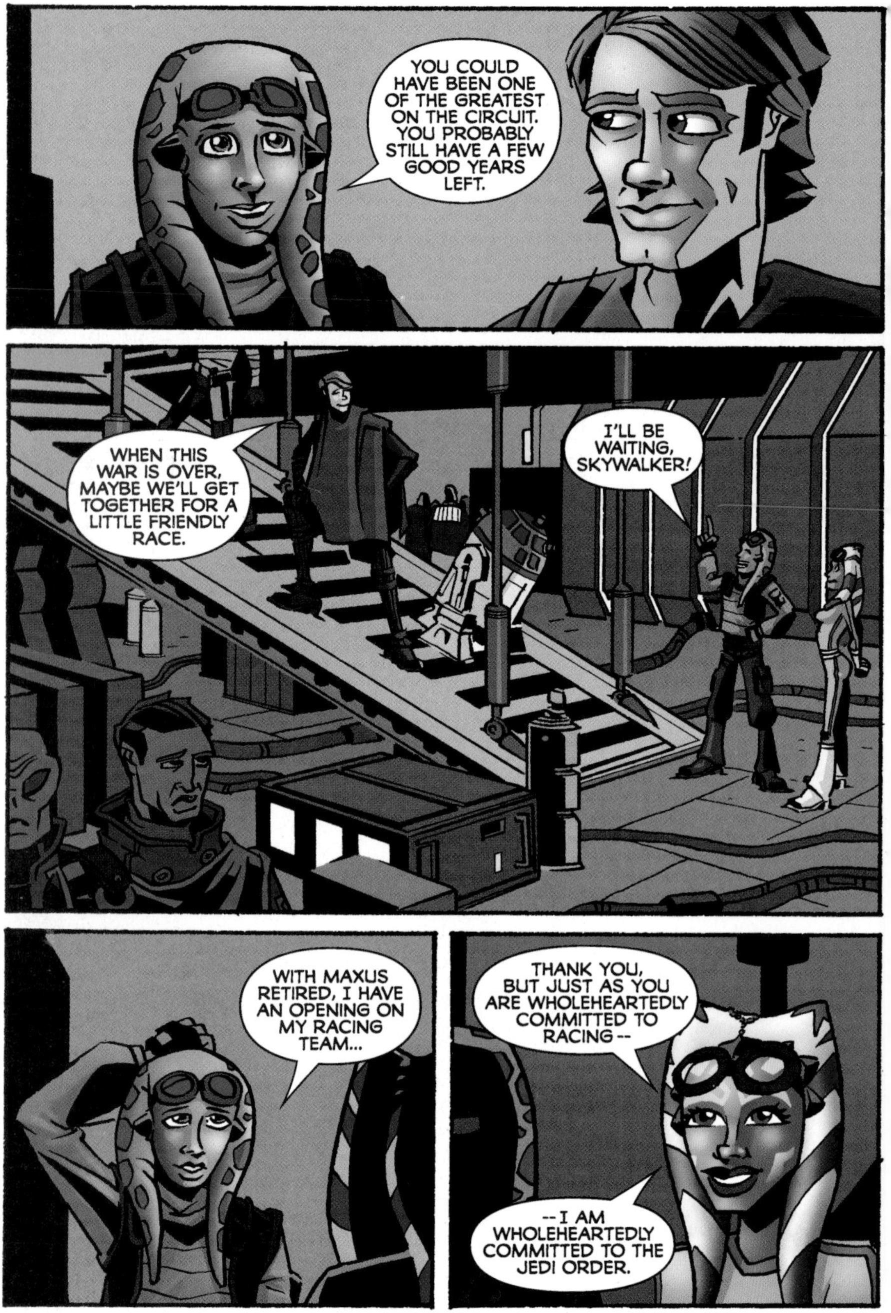
YOU COULD HAVE BEEN ONE OF THE GREATEST ON THE CIRCUIT. YOU PROBABLY STILL HAVE A FEW GOOD YEARS LEFT.
WHEN THIS WAR IS OVER, MAYBE WE'LL GET TOGETHER FOR A LITTLE FRIENDLY RACE.
I'LL BE WAITING, SKYWALKER!
WITH MAXUS RETIRED, I HAVE AN OPENING ON MY RACING TEAM...
THANK YOU, BUT JUST AS YOU ARE WHOLEHEARTEDLY COMMITTED TO RACING --
-- I AM WHOLEHEARTEDLY COMMITTED TO THE JEDI ORDER.

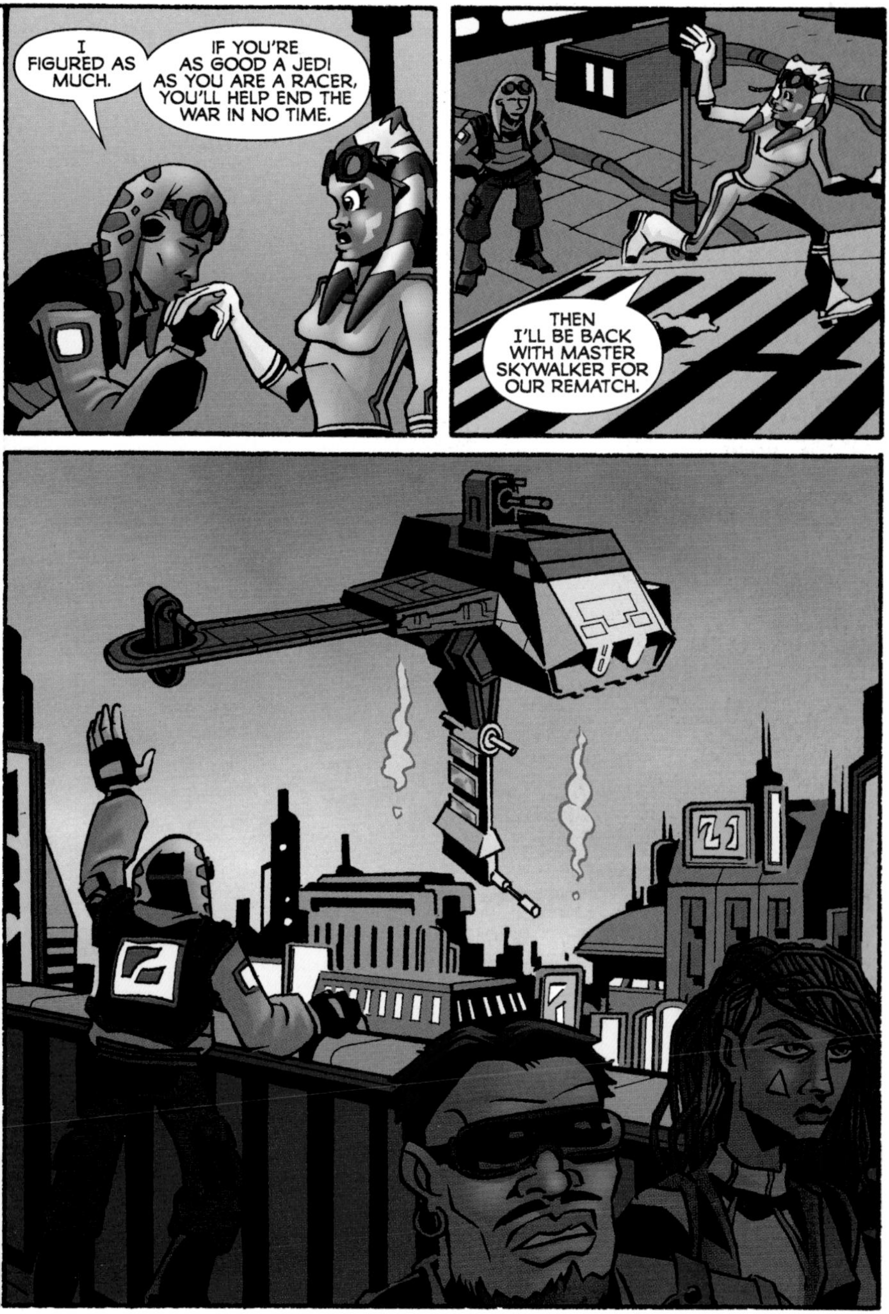
I FIGURED AS MUCH.
IF YOU'RE AS GOOD A JEDI AS YOU ARE A RACER, YOU'LL HELP END THE WAR IN NO TIME.
THEN I'LL BE BACK WITH MASTER SKYWALKER FOR OUR REMATCH.

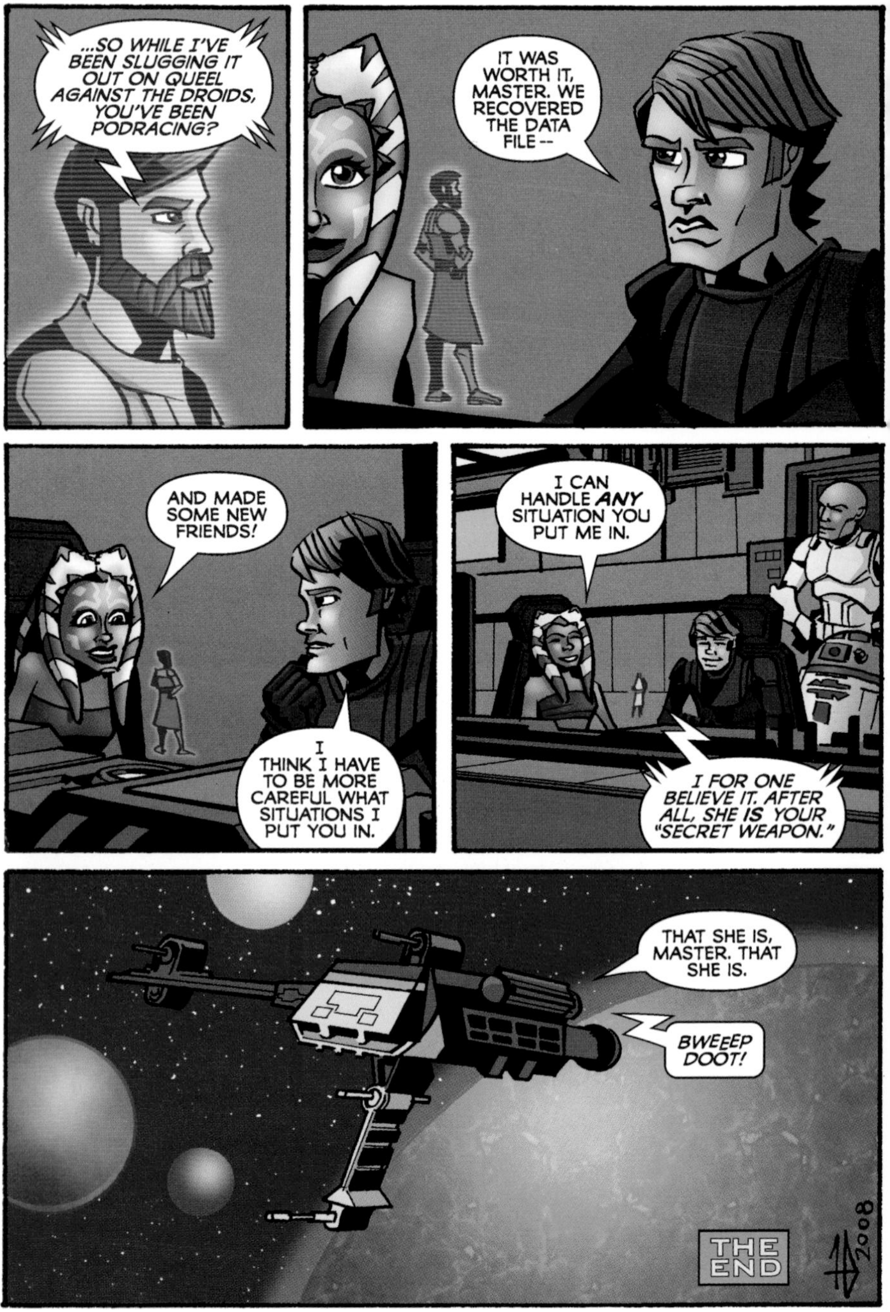
...SO WHILE I'VE BEEN SLUGGING IT OUT ON QUEEL AGAINST THE DROIDS, YOU'VE BEEN PODRACING?
IT WAS WORTH IT, MASTER. WE RECOVERED THE DATA FILE --
AND MADE SOME NEW FRIENDS!
I THINK I HAVE TO BE MORE CAREFUL WHAT SITUATIONS I PUT YOU IN.
I CAN HANDLE ANY SITUATION YOU PUT ME IN.
I FOR ONE BELIEVE IT. AFTER ALL, SHE IS YOUR "SECRET WEAPON."
THAT SHE IS, MASTER. THAT SHE IS.
BWEEEP DOOT!
THE END
2008

PRESIDENT AND PUBLISHER **MIKE RICHARDSON**

EXECUTIVE VICE PRESIDENT **NEIL HANKERSON**

CHIEF FINANCIAL OFFICER **TOM WEDDLE**

VICE PRESIDENT OF PUBLISHING **RANDY STRADLEY**

VICE PRESIDENT OF BUSINESS DEVELOPMENT **MICHAEL MARTENS**

VICE PRESIDENT OF MARKETING, SALES, AND LICENSING **ANITA NELSON**

VICE PRESIDENT OF PRODUCT DEVELOPMENT **DAVID SCROGGY**

VICE PRESIDENT OF INFORMATION TECHNOLOGY **DALE LAFOUNTAIN**

DIRECTOR OF PURCHASING **DARLENE VOGEL**

GENERAL COUNSEL **KEN LIZZI**

EDITORIAL DIRECTOR **DAVEY ESTRADA**

SENIOR MANAGING EDITOR **SCOTT ALLIE**

SENIOR BOOKS EDITOR, DARK HORSE BOOKS **CHRIS WARNER**

SENIOR BOOKS EDITOR, M PRESS/DH PRESS **ROB SIMPSON**

EXECUTIVE EDITOR **DIANA SCHUTZ**

DIRECTOR OF DESIGN AND PRODUCTION **CARY GRAZZINI**

ART DIRECTOR **LIA RIBACCHI**

DIRECTOR OF SCHEDULING **CARA NIECE**

CLONE WARS ADVENTURES

Don't miss any of the action-packed adventures of your favorite **STAR WARS**®
characters, available at comics shops and bookstores in a galaxy near you!

$6.95 each!

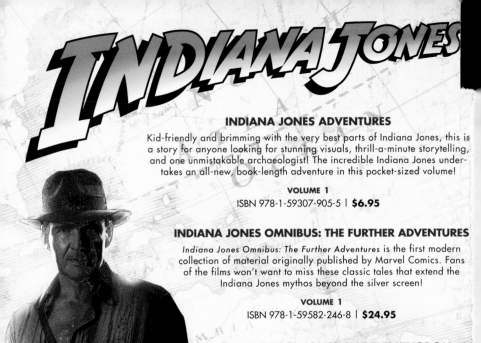

INDIANA JONES

INDIANA JONES ADVENTURES

Kid-friendly and brimming with the very best parts of Indiana Jones, this is a story for anyone looking for stunning visuals, thrill-a-minute storytelling, and one unmistakable archaeologist! The incredible Indiana Jones undertakes an all-new, book-length adventure in this pocket-sized volume!

VOLUME 1
ISBN 978-1-59307-905-5 | **$6.95**

INDIANA JONES OMNIBUS: THE FURTHER ADVENTURES

Indiana Jones Omnibus: The Further Adventures is the first modern collection of material originally published by Marvel Comics. Fans of the films won't want to miss these classic tales that extend the Indiana Jones mythos beyond the silver screen!

VOLUME 1
ISBN 978-1-59582-246-8 | **$24.95**

INDIANA JONES AND THE KINGDOM OF THE CRYSTAL SKULL TPB

The intrepid Doctor Henry Jones Jr. is back in his biggest adventure yet! The world-renowned archaeologist finds himself caught in a series of events that all point to a discovery unlike any other. But will his rivals in pursuit of this priceless treasure seize his quarry from right under his nose? Not if he, and a few unexpected companions, have anything to say about it!

ISBN 978-1-59307-952-9 | **$12.95**

INDIANA JONES OMNIBUS

Collecting many long-out-of-print stories in value-priced volumes, *Indiana Jones Omnibus* collections are a perfect jumping-on point for new readers!

VOLUME 1
ISBN 978-1-59307-887-4

VOLUME 2
ISBN 978-1-59307-953-6

$24.95 each!